T

DATE DUE

JS

GAYLORD

PRINTED IN U.S.A.

Adalbert Stifter's Late Prose

Studies in German Literature, Linguistics, and Culture

Edited by James Hardin
(South Carolina)

HELENA RAGG-KIRKBY

ADALBERT STIFTER'S
LATE PROSE

THE MANIA FOR MODERATION

CAMDEN HOUSE

First published 2000
by Camden House

Camden House is an imprint of Boydell & Brewer Inc.
PO Box 41026, Rochester, NY 14604–4126 USA
and of Boydell & Brewer Limited
PO Box 9, Woodbridge, Suffolk IP12 3DF, UK

ISBN: 1–57113–043–8

Library of Congress Cataloging-in-Publication Data

Ragg-Kirkby, Helena.
    Adalbert Stifter's late prose : the mania for moderation / Helena Ragg-Kirkby.
        p. cm. – (Studies in German literature, linguistics, and culture)
    Includes bibliographical references and index.
    ISBN 1–57113–043–8 (alk. paper)
        1. Stifter, Adalbert, 1805–1868—Criticism and interpretation. I. Title.
    II. Studies in German literature, linguistics, and culture (Unnumbered)

PT2525.Z5 R34 2000
833'.7—dc21
                                                                99-058827

A catalogue record for this title is available from the British Library.

This publication is printed on acid-free paper.
Printed in the United States of America

for
the four Hs

Contents

Acknowledgments

I AM PARTICULARLY GRATEFUL to the British Academy for funding my initial research on Stifter, and to the Adalbert Stifter Institut des Landes Oberösterreich for their generous support for this, its final outcome. My thanks also to Professor Martin Swales for his encouragement and for making numerous useful suggestions; Pamela Macfarlane, Elin Downes-Grainger, and Shaun Oldroyd; Caroline Anschütz; my family; and, finally, John Reddick (especially for the word monody).

Abbreviations

All page references to Stifter's works and letters are directly cited in the body of my text in abbreviated form. Those with a numerical prefix (e.g. "1,3: 251") relate to the *Historisch-kritische Gesamtausgabe*, ed. Doppler and Frühwald (Stuttgart: Kohlhammer, 1978–). The first two numbers indicate the relevant volume; the following numbers are page references. Other references are coded as follows:

Briefe   *Briefe*. Ed. Hans Schumacher (Zurich: Manesse, 1947)
FS   "Der fromme Spruch." In *Gesammelte Werke*. Ed. Konrad Steffen (Basel and Stuttgart: Birkhäuser, 1964)
GW   *Gesammelte Werke in sechs Bänden* (Frankfurt am Main: Insel, 1959)
MSB   *Die Mappe meines Urgroßvaters. Schilderungen. Briefe* (Munich: Winkler, 1968)
NS   *Der Nachsommer* (Munich: Winkler, 1978)

The orthography of the relevant edition is followed in all cases in the quotations, giving rise on occasion to divergent spellings, e.g. "erwiderte" (*MSB* 164) / "erwiederte" (5,1: 22).

The periodical *Vierteljahresschrift des Adalbert-Stifter-Institutes des Landes Oberösterreich* is abbreviated to VASILO in the Notes and Works Cited.

Introduction

The Unbridgeable Abyss

Ich fand mich einmal wieder in dem Entsetzlichen, Zugrunde-
richtenden. . . . Dann war Klingen, Verwirrung, Schmerz in meinen
Händen und Blut daran, die Mutter verband mich, und dann war ein
Bild, das so klar vor mir jetzt dasteht, als wäre es in reinlichen Farben
auf Porzellan gemalt. Ich stand in dem Garten, der von damals zuerst
in meiner Einbildungskraft ist, die Mutter war da, dann die andere
Großmutter, deren Gestalt in jenem Augenblicke auch zum ersten
Male in mein Gedächtnis kam, in mir war die Erleichterung, die alle
Male auf das Weichen des Entsetzlichen und Zugrunderichtenden
folgte, und ich sagte: "Mutter, da wächst ein Kornhalm."

Die Großmutter antwortete darauf: "Mit einem Knaben, der die
Fenster zerschlagen hat, redet man nicht." Ich verstand zwar den
Zusammenhang nicht, aber das Außerordentliche, das eben von mir
gewichen war, kam sogleich wieder; die Mutter sprach wirklich kein
Wort, und ich erinnere mich, daß ein ganz Ungeheures auf meiner
Seele lag, das mag der Grund sein, daß jener Vorgang noch jetzt in
meinem Innern lebt. (*MSB* 604)

ADALBERT STIFTER DIED ON 28 JANUARY 1868. The *Linzer Zeitung*
of the previous day had reported a "worsening" in the condition of
the "ailing Herr Hofrat Adalbert Stifter" and had claimed that he had
been given the last rites; it then reported the sad news that he had finally succumbed to cirrhosis of the liver.[1] In fact, Stifter had slit his
throat with a razor shortly after midnight on 26 January, had been
stitched up again, and had finally died after two days of agony.[2] At first
sight it might seem that such a gruesome and messy suicide was at odds
with a life that this famously gentle, pious, Catholic poet of nature described as being "as simple as a blade of corn." But, as the above extract
from his posthumously published autobiographical fragment "Mein Leben" (My Life) suggests, this was not the case. Here, Stifter recounts an
incident from his earliest years — and his primal experience is one of
fracture, terror, pain, alienation, impending destruction, "das Entsetzli-
che" and "das Zugrunderichtende." This is his first memory: a memory

of trauma, a look into the abyss at the very threshold of his life. A monstrous dimension ("ein . . . Ungeheueres") suddenly opens up beneath the surface harmony. His mother initially does what all mothers do and bandages his injured hands ("die Mutter verband mich") — but she then does the impossible, the unthinkable: she betrays him ("die Mutter sprach wirklich kein Wort"). Stifter's life began and ended with terrible wounds; the abyss opened up, and he spent his entire creative life trying in vain to close it.

Stifter was born on 23 October 1805 in the village of Oberplan (now Horní Plana) in southern Bohemia.[3] As a pupil at the local primary school, he was conspicuously intelligent; but when his father, a linen weaver and smallholder, died in 1817, Stifter left school to work in the family's fields. However, his maternal grandfather felt that the boy's talents were being wasted and took him to the Benedictine monastery of Kremsmünster in Upper Austria. After subjecting him to a somewhat unconventional entrance examination, Father Placidus Hall accepted him into the renowned monastic grammar school. Here, Stifter developed a talent for physics and astronomy as well as for literature and painting, and he chose to study law at the University of Vienna after he had passed through school with flying colours. But the unhappiness that would dominate his life had already set in. He disliked cities in general and Vienna in particular; he had little interest in the law (he would have preferred to become a landscape painter); he was forced to work as a private tutor in order to pay his rent (at one point, he taught physics and mathematics to Metternich's son); and yet could not return home due to the presence there of his loathed stepfather. His state of unhappiness was not helped by his love affair with Fanny Greipl. Their relationship was doomed from the outset, not least because her parents did not approve of this student with no prospects. Although Stifter renounced her, he continued to pine for her. He lost what little interest he had had in his studies; he failed to present himself to resit an examination; and he constantly had to move house in order to avoid the many people to whom he owed money. Despite his continuing devotion to Fanny, he married Amalia Mohaupt, a cleaner, in 1837. Although his letters are littered with declarations of his need for Amalia and of his delight in their solid bourgeois domesticity, Stifter seems to have felt no more fondness for her than she did for him. She was uneducated and unsympathetic to his writing. She was also sexually well-travelled, the polar opposite of Fanny. Stifter, a man of great appetites, seems to have been unable to resist Amalia's physical allure whilst simultaneously being disgusted by sexuality and continuing to worship the unavailable, virginal Fanny (to whom he was still declaring his love

after he was married). The only other benefit of Amalia to Stifter was that she took over the reins of the household. This enabled Stifter to begin to publish fiction, his first volume of short stories, *Studien* (Studies) appearing in 1844. His writing did not alleviate his financial problems, however, and his misery was compounded by his and Amalia's inability to have a child. After spending a year or so visiting Oberplan (1845) and Linz (1847), the couple adopted Amalia's lively niece, Juliane Mohaupt. In March 1848, Stifter was in Vienna and witnessed the beginning of the Revolution. He initially welcomed the liberation from the oppression of the Metternich era and even agreed to stand as a candidate in the Frankfurt parliament. But he was conservative by nature and soon began to fear the "immorality," chaos, and violence of the Revolution. He retreated to Linz where he continued to write short stories (*Bunte Steine* [Coloured Stones], 1853) and practise journalism, and he was also appointed Inspector of Primary Schools for Upper Austria. Despite this improvement in his professional standing, though, Stifter's personal life was showing signs of intolerable strain. He began to keep his *Tagebuch über Malereiarbeiten* (Diary of Painting, 1854–68), in which he listed in obsessive detail every hour and minute that he spent painting; the school text book he had written was rejected; he was involved in constant wrangles over money with his stepbrother; and, far worse, Juliane, aged barely eleven, ran away because she could no longer bear Amalia's constant beatings. She was found and returned to the family, but her unhappiness with the family was such that a few years later she ran away for the second time and drowned herself in the Danube. Stifter, the would-be guardian and educator of young minds, was mortified by the failure that this implied (he chose to blame the onset of menstruation for her act of "madness"), as well as by his feelings of grief and guilt. He and Amalia both began increasingly to suffer from hypochondria: he began to keep another diary, "Mein Befinden" (The State of My Health, 1864), in which he listed his symptoms in extravagant detail, from his appetite (or lack of it) right down to the colour and consistency of his faeces. Although Stifter had initially been keen to be appointed Inspector of Schools, he found it almost impossible to reconcile his civil service career with his creativity. Accordingly, he was relieved when he was pensioned off on the grounds of ill health in 1865 and awarded the title of "Hofrat." His remaining energies were devoted to the novel *Witiko* (1865–67); the two short stories "Der Kuß von Sentze" (The Kiss of Sentze) and "Der fromme Spruch" (The Pious Saying); and the final, lengthy version of "Die Mappe meines Urgroßvaters" (The Papers of My Great-Grandfather; published posthumously, as were the two stories).

One could perhaps be forgiven for seeing Stifter as an embodiment of the Biedermeier age in its most odiously cosy and narrow-minded form. And yet this man, insufferably pedantic, self-righteous, self-satisfied as he was in everyday life, was also a trailblazer far ahead of his time, and the writer of some of the most beautiful, poignant, and powerful prose in the German language.

A Mania for Moderation

Ever since Stifter first appeared in print, there has been no shortage of people ready to offer an opinion about his work.[4] The contemporary critical responses were initially favourable. The early *Studien* were generally acclaimed as a triumph for worthy values and had no less an admirer than Eichendorff, who praised Stifter's "geistige Auffassung der Liebe und das innige Verständnis der Natur," and rejoiced to find a body of writing quite uncontaminated by modernist excesses: "nicht eine Spur von moderner Zerrissenheit, von selbstgefälliger Frivolität oder moralisch experimentierender Selbstquälerei ist in dieser gesunden Poesie."[5] *Bunte Steine* was similarly well received in most quarters, as demonstrated by a gushing review in the Berlin *National-Zeitung*:

> Der Großvater oder die Großmutter im Verkehr mit den Enkelkindern, der arme kindliche Pfarrer, der Pechbrenner, allerlei wunderliches Volk, welches mit seinen harmlosen Eigenheiten ein unbekanntes Dasein führt, das sind die Personen, denen wir begegnen und für die uns Stifter umso mehr gewinnt, als er mit der gesundesten Frische, der liebevollsten Achtsamkeit und der treffendsten Unmittelbarkeit die intimsten Äußerungen ihres Wesens, ihres Charakters, ihrer Gemütswelt zeichnet.[6]

But the same years also saw Friedrich Hebbel's notorious attacks on Stifter: the mocking epigram that acted as a stimulus for Stifter to write his famous preface to *Bunte Steine*,[7] followed in due course by Hebbel's scathing criticism of Stifter's novel *Der Nachsommer* (Indian Summer, 1857) in which he promised the crown of Poland to anyone who had voluntarily read the novel right through to the end:

> Drei starke Bände! Wir glauben nichts zu riskieren, wenn wir demjenigen, der beweisen kann, daß er sie ausgelesen hat, ohne als Kunstrichter dazu verpflichtet zu sein, die Krone von Polen versprechen. Wir machen jedoch den Verfasser nur in geringem Grade für das mißratene Buch verantwortlich; er war sogleich bei seinem ersten Auftreten Manierist und mußte, verhätschelt, wie er wurde, zuletzt natürlich alles Maß verlieren. . . . es fehlt nur noch die Betrachtung

der Wörter, womit man schildert, und die Schilderung der Hand, womit man diese Betrachtung niederschreibt, so ist der Kreis vollendet.[8]

What is striking about these views is that, love him or loathe him, no one questioned what Stifter represented: he was simply the high priest of "Maß" (moderation), tranquillity, unambiguous normality, the organic bond between man and nature, the happy family and community, the transcendent nature of "die Dinge" ("things"). In the closing decades of the nineteenth century, however, the picture began to change — thanks in no small part to Friedrich Nietzsche. In *Menschliches, Allzumenschliches* (Human, All Too Human, 1879), he vaunted *Der Nachsommer* as one of only very few German novels that deserved to be read more than once:

> Wenn man von Goethe's Schriften absieht . . . : was bleibt eigentlich von der deutschen Prosa-Litteratur übrig, das es verdiente, wieder und wieder gelesen zu werden? Lichtenberg's Aphorismen, das erste Buch von Jung-Stilling's Lebensgeschichte, Adalbert Stifter's Nachsommer und Gottfried Keller's Leute von Seldwyla, — und damit wird es einstweilen am Ende sein.[9]

It is perhaps no coincidence that one of Nietzsche's disciples, namely Ernst Bertram, subsequently perceived hidden depths in Stifter's fiction. In his 1907 book *Studien zu Adalbert Stifters Novellentechnik*, he suggested that Stifter's emphatic avoidance of passion could be derived only from an excess of it.[10] In 1939, Fritz Klatt took this further and argued that the very essence of Stifter lay in a kind of wild extremism that he desperately struggled to conceal and tame.[11] Only ten years later, Thomas Mann remarked:

> Man hat oft den Gegensatz hervorgekehrt zwischen Stifters blutig-selbstmörderischem Ende und der edlen Sanftmut seines Dichtertums. Seltener ist beobachtet worden, daß hinter der stillen, innigen Genauigkeit gerade seiner Naturbetrachtung eine Neigung zum Exzessiven, Elementar-Katastrophalen, Pathologischen wirksam ist. . . . Stifter ist einer der merkwürdigsten, hintergründigsten, heimlich kühnsten und wunderlich packendsten Erzähler der Weltliteratur, kritisch viel zu wenig ergründet.[12]

Written at around the same time, Erik Lunding's study *Adalbert Stifter: Mit einem Anhang über Kierkegaard und die existentielle Wissenschaft* (1946) retains its status even today as one of the most radical new departures in Stifter criticism. In more detail than anyone before him, he identified submerged conflicts and fears in Stifter's life and fiction, with particular reference to existentialism. Of course, modern literary criticism owes at least as much to Freud as to the Existentialists,

and Freudian theory, although all too frequently ham-fistedly applied (most egregiously in Alfred Winterstein's *Adalbert Stifter: Persönlichkeit und Werk. Eine tiefenpsychologische Studie*, 1946), has been of some use in helping critics to chart the submerged terrain (Michael Kaiser's 1971 study *Adalbert Stifter: Eine literaturpsychologische Untersuchung seiner Erzählungen* is worth noting in this respect, as is the 1960s work of Kurt Gerhard Fischer). However, perhaps the most ground-breaking work on Stifter has emerged since the 1970s and relies on close reading of the texts rather than on any "-isms." By using this approach, Hans Dietrich Irmscher, John Reddick, Martin and Erika Swales and Helen Watanabe-O'Kelly have emphatically destabilised the traditional view of Stifter (which, interestingly, the publications of the Adalbert-Stifter-Institut in Linz still largely seek to uphold). I am clearly indebted to these critics who have opened countless doors on Stifter's fiction. However, even their work shares one major limitation with the vast majority of Stifter criticism: it has invariably concentrated only on the author's prose of the 1840s and 1850s, so that one could almost be led to believe that *Der Nachsommer* was his final work. Yet the fiction of this relatively early period cannot and should not be viewed in isolation. It is true that stories such as "Der Hochwald" (The Alpine Forest, 1844), "Brigitta" (Brigitta, 1847), "Der Hagestolz" (The Recluse, 1850), "Bergkristall" (Rock Crystal, 1853), "Kalkstein" (Limestone, 1853), "Turmalin" (Tourmaline, 1853), and "Granit" (Granite, 1853) are far more readily accessible than later ones such as "Der fromme Spruch," "Der Kuß von Sentze," *Die Letzte Mappe* and *Witiko* — not least because there is no plot of any substance in these latter stories. Even in Stifter's lifetime, they were dismissed by reviewers and friends who were both disappointed and embarrassed by his apparently failing powers as a writer. Although I have called this book a study of Stifter's later fiction, his oeuvre in fact needs to be considered as a whole, since the only difference between the early, relatively popular stories and his problematic later ones is one of mode: the essential concerns remain the same throughout his literary career.

If Stifter's work is taken as a whole, it soon becomes clear that its power derives from the tension between the surface and the depths, between moderation and mania. Some of the newer critics have tended to dismiss the surface as empty pretence, as a mask that has to be destroyed; those who seek to preserve Stifter's traditional reputation do the opposite, and dismiss all talk of subtexts as stuff and nonsense. Both are mistaken: it is the dual perspective afforded by text and subtext that gives Stifter's fiction the "magic" detected in it by Thomas Mann.[13] And, whilst I am certainly not going to offer a "psychobiography," it is

nonetheless striking that this tension is evident in Stifter's own life as well as in his art. In 1853, Heinrich Reitzenbeck gave a sentimental account of Stifter as a man, declaring that his character consisted in "reverence for religion, morals, law, and truth."[14] Stifter would no doubt have agreed. In a letter to his publisher Gustav Heckenast of 25 May 1848 he claims to be wholly given to moderation: "Ich bin ein Mann des Maßes" (*MSB* 686). Yet this self-styled Man of Moderation kept the two diaries mentioned above ("Tagebuch über Malereiarbeiten" and "Mein Befinden"); obsessively revised what he had already written (with the result that practically all his stories exist in two versions, a *Journal-* and a *Buchfassung*[15]); obsessively counted the number of letters (*sic!*) in each draft of these stories[16]; and eventually slit his own throat. His writings display the same tension. In both his letters and his fiction, he continually emphasises his ideal of moderation and self-restraint. All human greatness appears to depend on the fulfilment of this ideal, whether it be at the level of individuals, of peoples, or even of entire empires.[17] Even artistic greatness apparently lies in moderation: in one of his (immoderate) attacks on Hebbel, Stifter proclaims:

> In diese rohe und ungeklärte, auch niemals gemäßigte und gebändigte Last ist *nicht der schwächste Strahl des Schönen gedrungen*, daher dieses Ergehen im Ungeheuerlichen, im Absonderlichen, in ganz von jedem Maß Abweichenden, was wie Kraft aussehen soll, aber in der Tat Schwäche ist: denn das Merkmal jeder Kraft ist Maß, Beherrschung, sittliche Organisierung. (*Briefe*, 125; Stifter's emphasis)

Beneath the tranquil surfaces of every one of Stifter's own texts, however, is precisely what he claimed to despise in Hebbel: all that is "monstrous," "strange," and "deviant," a vision of a world devoid of moderation or measure. Time and time again in his earlier writing he explicitly confronts us with all that is *not* moderate: the abyss opens up "ohne Maß und Grenze" (1,4: 27), and passion bursts forth "ohne Maß und ohne Grenzen" (1,4: 64), "ohne Maß und Ende" (1,5: 454), "unmäßig" (1,4: 77), "über alles Maß" (1,4: 348). It is telling indeed that Stifter wrote to Heckenast in despair of "diesen Zwiespalt in meinem Innern" (*MSB* 686).

Let us return to the fiction. In the earlier stories, the split between the two perspectives of "Maß" and "Unmaß" is frequently conveyed through images of surface and depth — the surface benign and blessed, the depths filthy, chaotic, even deathly. "Kalkstein" offers an eloquent example of this kind of imagery. After the storm rages over the Kar, the area becomes flooded and the perfect mirror-like surface of the water conduces to an image of comprehensive harmony and bliss:

> Die große Wasserfläche glänzte unter den Strahlen der Sonne, sie
> machte zu dem Grün der Wiese und dem Grau der Steine den dritten
> stimmenden und schimmernden Klang, und der Steg stand abenteu-
> erlich wie eine dunkle Linie über dem silbernen Spiegel. (2,2: 86)

But hidden beneath this beautiful surface lie dangerous depths and pit-
falls, invisible through the murky water ("das Wasser bei Überschwem-
mungen sei trüb, und lasse die Tiefe und Ungleichheit des Bodens
unter sich nicht bemerken," 2,2: 92); indeed, the "filthiness" beneath
the shimmering surface makes the floodwaters potentially fatal:

> Wenn nun das Karufer überschwemmt ist, und [die Kinder] von dem
> Stege in das Wasser gehen, so können manche in eine Grube oder
> eine Vertiefung geraten, und dort verunglüken; denn das kothige
> Wasser der Überschwemmung läßt den Boden nicht sehen. (2,2: 128)

In the story "Zwei Schwestern" (Two Sisters, 1850), it is a chasm —
one of Stifter's central images — that is rendered invisible on the surface: "Die Furche aber war nicht zu sehen, da die ganze Spalte, wie
überall an den Ufern dieses Sees mit dichtem Gebüsche und mit
schlanken wuchernden Bäumen bedeckt war" (1,6: 255). The idea of a
latent landscape submerged by water recurs in *Der Nachsommer*, where
Heinrich paints a canvas in which submarine mountains are mutedly
visible ("ein Bild . . . in welchem sich die Berge, die den See umstan-
den, sichtbar auch unter der Wasserfläche fortsetzten, und nur durch
einen tieferen Ton gedämpft waren," *NS* 324–5). In another story,
"Die Narrenburg" (The Castle of Fools, 1844), the unfathomable
Chelion is depicted through an image combining pure white surface
and black, uliginous depths: "da war sie weiß, ehe sie gestorben ist, so
weiß war sie, wie die Lilien, die unten im Sumpfe wachsen, und die
Häupter auf das schwarze Wasser legen" (1,4: 387). In "Der Hochwald," it is the scattered notes played by Clarissa on her harp that point
to a submerged landscape: "einzelne Töne . . . , die nicht zusammen-
hängen, oder Inselspitzen einer untergesunkenen Melodie sind" (1,4:
219).

The dual perspective in "Der Hochwald" is in fact particularly eloquent, as not only the reader but also the characters themselves are
faced with contradictory pictures of a single reality. As Reddick has argued,[18] one of the most revealing and poignant examples of this technique is the point in the story where the sisters return for yet another
telescopic glimpse of their father's castle — only to see that their distant
home has become a charred ruin. Through the telescope, the girls are
given a vision of all-engulfing chaos, catastrophe and filth; but opposed

to this is the larger vista apparent to the naked eye, a vista within which the chaos is such a tiny blip that it is simply not visible at all:

> Clarissa warf sich neuerdings vor das Glas, und sah lange hinein — aber dieselbe eine Botschaft war immer darinnen, doppelt ängstend durch dieselbe stumme Einförmigkeit und Klarheit. Auch Johanna sah hindurch, um ihn nur gewöhnen zu können, den drohenden unheimlichen Anblick; denn sobald sie das Auge wegwendete, und den schönen blauen Waldduft sah, wie sonst, und den lieblich blauen Würfel, wie sonst, und den lachenden blauen Himmel gar so prangend, so war es ihr, als könne es ja ganz und gar nicht möglich sein — und wenn sie wieder in das Glas sah, so war's, als sei selbst das heitre Firmament düster und schreckhaft, und das Walddunkel ein riesig hinausgehendes schwarzes Bahrtuch. (1,4: 307–8)

Which view is true? The blessed, blue, benign one, or the black, abyssal, terrifying one? Both. The girls are not misreading the signs or distorting a single, true picture: there is no one "truth." Evidently, such images as this are by no means manneristic embellishments. On the contrary: they are the core of Stifter's works, conveying a vision in which the world exists for us only as interpretations and perspectives. As the grandfather in "Granit" warns us: "Es ist kein sicherer Halt möglich" (2,2: 41).

Of course, this tendency to open everything up to multiple interpretation has crucial implications for Stifter's symbolic mode. On one level, Stifter clearly does want to offer a comfortingly unambiguous, one-to-one equivalence of meaning; but his symbols bespeak the knowledge, or maybe the fear, that in a world that is ultimately dependent on multiple perspectives, the unequivocal symbol is no longer possible. This being so, one of the most poignant aspects of his fiction is the way in which so many of the characters try to surround themselves with tokens of wholeness, of thereness, of intrinsic meaning. Needless to say, the urge to collect such tokens was nothing unusual in the nineteenth century. This was the great age of taxonomy and system-building that had developed as a response to political, social and natural events as much as to "scientific" progress. Roget's *Thesaurus*, itself an elaborately taxonomic "collection" of words in the English language, was published in the same year as *Bunte Steine*.[19] Freud would dedicate himself to systematising the human psyche not long after Stifter's death, and the two crucial texts of the era were dedicated to the ordering of classes: *On the Origin of Species* and *The Communist Manifesto*.[20] Stifter is very much a part of this prevailing sense that the world could be fathomed and ordered, named and controlled. It is in this light that I also understand his characters' tendency to structure their fictive lives around particular rituals. As I shall demonstrate, the ritual in Stifter's

fiction that recurs most frequently is that of cleaning, but various others are striking: the old uncle's locking rituals in "Der Hagestolz," the ceremony with which the "Kalkstein" priest treats his linen, Risach's ritual behaviour in *Der Nachsommer*. All seem to suggest the ways in which humans can order and regulate their lives. At the same time, however, Stifter's fiction shows the ways in which both collecting and ritual behaviour become manic attempts to *evade* existence rather than to order and comprehend it. In stories such as "Der Hagestolz," "Kalkstein," "Der Waldsteig" (The Forest Path, 1850), "Der Waldgänger" (The Forest Walker, 1847), and particularly in the novel *Der Nachsommer*, we witness characters who hoard possession after possession and obsessively create orderly lives for themselves — only ultimately to betray a manic anxiety about the shattered nature of existence. These "things" and patterns of behaviour become part of a will for moderation, for measure, for ultimate meaning; a will so fervent that it betrays mania. In *Witiko* and "Der fromme Spruch," however, we no longer encounter manic collectors, or zealous washerwomen scrubbing away at potential filth. Instead, Stifter's medium becomes his message: his *style* itself becomes a ritual, conveying exactly the same anxiety as the actions of the characters in the early stories.

If we view *Witiko* in this light, it is surprising that the novel has been so widely ignored, dismissed and disparaged. Although it has suffered from this conspicuous neglect by both nineteenth- and twentieth-century critics it is surely Stifter's *extreme* masterpiece — one seemingly far removed from his earliest published work, the story "Der Condor" (The Condor, 1844), but differing from it only in mode, not in its essential burden. "Der Condor" is cluttered with paraphernalia: noble women crying into cushions, clever males doing manly things with scientific apparatus, accomplished but humble heroes soaring free as a bird. But in the same story we find one of Stifter's finest evocations of a world beyond measure and moderation. As the hot-air balloon soars upward, Cornelia is confronted by a panoply of clouds that suggest to those on the ground warm, glowing "Morgenrosen"; but viewed from the sky, these very clouds are "weiß schimmernde Eisländer . . . in den furchtbar blauen Bächen der Luft schwimmend, und mit Schlünden und Spalten dem Schiffe entgegen starrend." Cornelia is far beyond anything she has previously known: she looks down at her nurturing, secure home, the earth ("das gewohnte Mutterantlitz"; "das wohlbekannte Vaterhaus"), but it is cold and alien: "alles war fremd und die vertraute Wohnlichkeit derselben war schon nicht mehr sichtbar, und mithin auch nicht die Fäden, die uns an ein theures, kleines Fleckchen binden, das wir Heimath nennen." Again, a double perspective is ap-

plied to the clouds. Seen from the earth, they are "Silberschäfchen des Himmels." Once the Condor reaches the "höchsten Aether," however, these "sweet little lambs" have turned into heaving, ghostly images of death and burial: "weiße, dünne, sich dehnende und regende Leichentücher." Stricken with fear, Cornelia turns for reassurance to the heavens, "die schöne blaue Glocke unserer Erde," but Heaven has ceased to exist, and she sees only a chasm: "ein ganz schwarzer Abgrund . . . , ohne Maß und Grenze in die Tiefe gehend." The stars come out, but they are distant, isolated and cold: "winzige, ohnmächtige Goldpunkte, verloren durch die Oede gestreut." Meanwhile, the radiant sun, the bringer of light and warmth, has become "ein drohendes Gestirn, ohne Wärme, ohne Strahlen, eine scharfgeschnittene Scheibe aus wallendem, blähendem, weißgeschmolzenem Metalle," and it stares "mit vernichtendem Glanze aus dem Schlunde — und doch nicht einen Hauch des Lichtes festhaltend in diesen wesenlosen Räumen." While Cornelia's two fellow (male) passengers pursue their business, oblivious to everything but their scientific data, she is transported to a zone of absolute otherness where even silence has died ("Rings ausgestorbene Stille"; "auch das Reich des Klanges war hier oben aus"), a zone replete with terrible nothingness: "nichts, nichts da, als die entsetzlichen Sterne." Yet this "luftiger Abgrund" is at one and the same time "unsere zarte, liebe Luft, in der sie schifften — dieselbe Luft, die morgen die Wangen eines Säuglings fächelt" (1,4: 23–8). Compared with the perspective of her scientist companions or of ordinary folk living their ordinary lives on *terra firma*, Cornelia's vision may seem a temporary aberration, a localised blemish on a larger canvas suggestive of iconic wholeness; and yet it throws the entire canvas sharply into question. In contrast to "Der Condor," *Witiko* is quite devoid of paraphernalia, indeed it is devoid of practically everything save its mesmeric, litaneutical style. However, we shall see that the vision of the abyss in *Witiko* is even more drastic than in "Der Condor" because Stifter attempts to stifle it completely — and by trying to stifle it, expresses it all the more emphatically. In "Der Condor" the abyss is located and thereby localised; in *Witiko* it is omnipresent. Beneath the surface of Biedermeier solidity is a vision of fracture, emptiness, meaninglessness not only more radical than that of any other nineteenth-century author, but more radical than the vision of any twentieth-century author, precisely because there is such a disjuncture between text and sub-text. Stifter simply leaves the future behind.

Naturally, we as readers cannot hope to chart the submerged landscapes any more than Stifter himself could; we, too, can only ever aspire to an interpretation of Stifter's interpretations. In *Witiko*, Wentila

comments that Benno is constantly searching for ultimate truths
("sucht Alles zu ergründen, was einmal geschehen ist," 5,2: 231) —
but this search will never end. The texts are constructed in such a way
that all the central concerns are ultimately rendered unfathomably, un-
speakably ambiguous — and this is a reflection of the world in which
we live. This is not to say that the possibility of ultimate answers is entirely ruled out; Stifter does imply this, but never quite dares to say so
openly. He must keep his fingers crossed, *just in case*:

> Ob es je dahin kommen wird, ob noch Millionen Jahre verfließen, bis
> es dahin kommt — wer kann das wissen: aber streben müssen wir
> danach, als Ziel muß es immerfort und leuchtend vor unseren Augen
> schweben. (*GW* VI: 393)

His heir and successor Franz Kafka could hardly have put it better:
"Wenn auch keine Erlösung kommt, so will ich doch jeden Augenblick
ihrer würdig sein."[21]

Notes

[1] See Kurt Gerhard Fischer, *Adalbert Stifters Leben und Werk in Briefen und
Dokumenten* (Frankfurt am Main: Fischer, 1962), 668.

[2] As there have traditionally been, broadly speaking, two sharply opposed
"camps" in Stifter criticism, it is not surprising that critics have failed to agree
on how Stifter died. Hermann Augustin, for example, claims that the very
idea that the author committed suicide is based on "hearsay" (*Adalbert Stifters Krankheit und Tod: Eine biographische Quellenstudie* [Basel/Stuttgart:
Schwabe, 1964], 136). He offers some unconvincing, not to say comical explanations for Stifter's death, such as a shaving accident (135–6): he argues
that Stifter might simply have fallen and landed with his throat against the razor blade (137). See also Hermann Augustin, "Ärztliches zu Adalbert Stifters
Tod," *VASILO* 8 (1959): 19–34. Andreas Markus, however, takes it as a fact
that Stifter committed suicide (*Der Tod Adalbert Stifters* [Neudeln: Ebering,
1967], 5). See also Wolfgang Matz, *Adalbert Stifter oder "Diese fürchterliche
Wendung der Dinge"* (Munich and Vienna: Hanser, 1995).

[3] For biographical details, see in particular Alois Raimund Hein, *Adalbert
Stifter: Sein Leben und seine Werke* (Vienna: Walter Krieg, 1952); Urban
Roedl, *Adalbert Stifter: Geschichte seines Lebens* (Bern: Francke, 1958), and
Adalbert Stifter in Selbstzeugnissen und Bilddokumenten (Reinbek bei Ham-
burg: Rowohlt, 1965); Martin and Erika Swales, *Adalbert Stifter: A Critical
Study* (Cambridge: Cambridge UP, 1984); Helen Watanabe-O'Kelly (trans.),
Adalbert Stifter: "Brigitta" and Other Tales (London: Penguin, 1990); Matz,
Adalbert Stifter.

[4] The responses of Stifter's contemporaries to his work are best documented by Moriz Enzinger, *Adalbert Stifter im Urteil seiner Zeit* (Vienna: Böhlau, 1968). The responses to the *Bunte Steine* collection of stories are usefully synthesised in the relevant *Apparat/Kommentar* volumes of the *Historisch-kritische Gesamtausgabe*. See 2,3: 52–64, 83–90, 270–2, 371–5, 415–18; and 2,4: 68–74, 177–9, 222.

[5] Cited in Enzinger, *Stifter im Urteil seiner Zeit,* 84.

[6] Cited in Enzinger, *Stifter im Urteil seiner Zeit,* 171.

[7] See Friedrich Hebbel, *Werke,* ed. Fricke, Keller and Pörnbacher (Munich: Hanser, 1965), vol. 3, 122.

[8] Hebbel, *Werke,* vol. 3, 682–3. Interestingly, another author — Theodor Storm — mocked Hebbel's mockery and claimed that he had found it easy to earn the crown of Poland. However, even Storm went on to say that he, like the vast majority of readers, had abandoned *Witiko* in despair: "Dagegen blieb ich stecken im *Witiko*" (cited in Enzinger, *Stifter im Urteil seiner Zeit,* 348).

[9] Friedrich Nietzsche, *Menschliches, Allzumenschliches,* in Friedrich Nietzsche, *Werke,* ed. Colli and Montinari (Berlin: de Gruyter, 1967), vol. 2, 237. For comments on Nietzsche's love of Stifter, see Ernst Bertram, *Nietzsche: Versuch einer Mythologie* (Bonn: Bouvier, 1965), 248; and Ernst Bertram, "Nietzsche die Briefe Adalbert Stifters lesend," *Ariadne: Jahrbuch der Nietzsche-Gesellschaft* (1925): 8.

[10] Ernst Bertram, *Studien zu Adalbert Stifters Novellentechnik* (Dortmund: Ruhfus, 1907), 31–2.

[11] "Die Grundstruktur von Adalbert Stifters Wesen ist eine mit allen Mitteln verdeckte und gebändigte Maßlosigkeit" (Fritz Klatt, "Stifter und das Dämonische," *Dichtung und Volkstum,* 40 [1939]: 276).

[12] Thomas Mann, "Die Entstehung des Doktor Faustus," in Thomas Mann, *Schriften und Reden zur Literatur, Kunst und Philosophie* (Frankfurt am Main and Hamburg: Fischer, 1968), vol. 3, 157–8.

[13] Thomas Mann, *Briefe 1937–47,* ed. Erika Mann (Frankfurt am Main: Fischer, 1963), 458.

[14] Cited in Fischer, *Leben und Werk,* 293.

[15] Stifter's stories mostly appeared first in the periodicals that were especially popular from the 1820s until the 1848 Revolution. Not long after publishing the stories in this form, Stifter began to revise them extensively and to publish them as separate volumes. Thus he was publishing new stories in the periodicals whilst simultaneously publishing the revised older stories as collections. Before the publication of the *Historisch-kritische Gesamtausgabe*, the two versions were known as the "Urfassungen" ("Original Versions") and "Studienfassungen" ("Study Versions"). Since the publication of the new

edition, however, they have generally been referred to as the "Journalfas-sungen" ("Journal Versions") and "Buchfassungen" ("Book Versions").

[16] See 2,3: 39.

[17] See *MSB* 687, 914; *GW* VI: 340, 365.

[18] John Reddick, "Mystification, Perspectivism and Symbolism in *Der Hoch-wald*," in *Adalbert Stifter heute,* ed. Johann Lachinger, Alexander Stillmark, and Martin Swales (Linz: Adalbert-Stifter-Institut des Landes Oberösterreich, 1985), 42.

[19] See Peter Mark Roget, *Roget's Thesaurus of English Words and Phrases: New Edition Completely Revised and Modernised*, ed. Robert A. Dutch (Longman: Harlow, 1962; first published 1852), xxiii.

[20] For an excellent introduction to the nineteenth-century obsession with the creation of systems see John Reddick, *Georg Büchner: The Shattered Whole* (Oxford: Oxford UP, 1994), 15–25.

[21] Franz Kafka, *Tagebücher*, in Franz Kafka, *Schriften. Tagebücher. Briefe: Kri-tische Ausgabe*, ed. Born et al. ([Frankfurt am Main]: Fischer, 1990), 376. I am indebted to Jost Schillemeit for locating the precise source of this quota-tion.

1: Rituals and Sublimations

"Zur Unruhe mehrten sich viele Dinge"
("Der Waldsteig")

" A LS KNABE TRUG ICH außer Ruthen Gesträuchen und Blüthen, die mich ergözten, auch noch andere Dinge nach Hause," writes Adalbert Stifter, adopting his most disingenuously unassuming tone in the introduction to *Bunte Steine*. "Dieser Sammelgeist nun ist noch immer nicht von mir gewichen" (2,2: 17–18).[1] Such a love of collecting was by no means exceptional in the 1850s, when these lines were published. Quite the opposite: Stifter's statement was strongly representative of his era in this respect. His interests, namely fine cuisine, collecting and restoring furniture and various other knick-knacks, owning dogs, and growing cacti, reflect the bourgeois predilection for material comfort and for the cultivation of nature that characterised the Austro-Hungarian Empire of the mid-nineteenth century.[2] Even when it appears that Stifter's stories are far removed from his contemporary reality (as, for example, seems most particularly to be the case in *Witiko*, which is set in twelfth-century Bohemia), the Biedermeier age with its classic values of stability, self-control, solid order, and mastery over nature provides the backdrop for his writing.

But Stifter was not simply a product of the Biedermeier culture and its ethos of order, moderation, and comfortable morality. As both a man and an artist, he was an heir to the ideas of the eighteenth century: to the Enlightenment, with its emphasis on reason, calm reflection, control, and categorisation, and to German Classicism, with its faith in transcendence and essence. It seems on one level to be clear that collecting is for Stifter a part of this, the legacy of Schiller and Goethe, Herder and Kant. This much we can infer from his term "Sammelgeist," the word "Geist" being clearly intended to affirm the moral and spiritual value of collecting. Not only does Stifter suggest that he himself is endowed with the virtues of solidity and stability enshrined in this "Sammelgeist": he also appears to attribute a similar immutability to his seemingly exemplary characters, many of whom, such as the "Kalkstein" priest, the Major in "Brigitta," von Risach in *Der Nachsommer*, Tiburius Kneigt in "Der Waldsteig," are tireless collectors, be it of exquisite linen, fine furniture, or specimens from nature.[3]

I now need to turn to the texts in order to show the ways in which Stifter uses the "collecting" motif apparently to maintain his overt faith in reason and the "Überblik über ein Größeres" that, according to the *Bunte Steine* preface, is the sovereign perspective that allows humans to comprehend the workings of the world (2,2: 15). As is evident from a comparison of the two versions of any of Stifter's stories, he tends to transfer the narrative focus from the characters (in the journal versions) to the physical objects which they collect (in the book versions). In "Turmalin," for instance, the descriptive weight falls on the couple's home as evoked through a catalogue of objects, whereas in its predecessor, "Der Pförtner im Herrenhause," the emphasis of the opening sequence falls on the characters, particularly Dall. This list of possessions in "Turmalin" can itself be seen in the context of the *Bunte Steine* preface as an attempt to purge the narrative of all vestiges of human interest, to deny the significance of the dynamic forces in man by turning away from their more overt gestures and turning instead towards plain objects — as an attempt to establish objectivity in all senses of the word. On the face of it, these objects appear to have an unproblematic, reliable existence for Stifter, and therefore seem to function as bastions of security and meaning that afford protection against the beguiling pyrotechnics of human passions. More generally, however, Stifter's emphasis on objects is one aspect of a crucial movement from orderless fluidity to orderly stasis that characterises the development of his entire oeuvre as well as his revisions of individual works. Significantly, the objects that the characters collect are more often than not inanimate, contributing to the sense of praiseworthy stasis that appears to reach its apotheosis in *Der Nachsommer*. Here, Heinrich Drendorf's collections include minerals and etchings; Risach and Mathilde both cherish their collections of wood; and Heinrich's father accumulates "geschnittene Steine" (*NS* 397), a detail which reminds us of Stifter's own fondness for "Steine und Erddinge" (2,2: 17).

Even on the surface, though, collecting does not serve the maintenance of equilibrium alone. The "Sammelgeist" is equally connected with repose and with the calming influence that the observation of objects exerts over man. This point is taken up by Walter Höllerer. He suggests that man finds peace through recognising the orderliness of objects ("Ruhe"; "Ordnung im Ding"), and he then adduces "Der Waldsteig" as a typical example of a story where inanimate objects function for the characters as "Ruhepunkte."[4] The same connection between tranquil reflection and collecting is made explicit by Stifter in *Der Nachsommer*. After starting his collection of engravings, Heinrich comments: "Ich lernte die Feinheiten die Großartigkeit die Schönheit

die Ruhe in der Behandlung immer mehr kennen und würdigen" (*NS* 361; my emphasis). Of course, *Ruhe* does not radiate solely from this collection. Throughout the whole novel, a similar aura of orderly calm emanates from the walls of its outwardly idyllic focal point, the *Rosenhaus*. We witness what is surely the ultimate in Stifterian gradualness as we, along with Heinrich, are made to observe through Risach's special lens the infinitesimal changes in the cactus until it eventually flowers, six hundred and five pages into the novel. Patient watching, patient waiting, "nichts im Übermaß" (*NS* 309): these are the imperatives in a world where everything can apparently be understood, and where man's role is to support the leading part played by objects.

As the example of the cactus makes clear, the characters' urge to collect is by no means limited to the actual objects themselves: in suitable cases they can devote themselves to the avid collection of data as well. Thus Heinrich busily measures and re-measures the depth of the lake; and it comes as no real surprise to find Stifter describing himself in the essay "Wiener Wetter" (Viennese Weather, 1844) as a supremely dedicated "weather collector" ("ob es noch irgendwo zwei emsigere Wetterbeobachter, Klassifizierer, Kenner und Wettersammler gibt, als mich und meinen Freund Grimbucker, lasse ich dahin gestellt sein," *MSB* 406–7).[5] Furthermore, in order to collect data there is every excuse to collect instruments, too, and so we find Risach taking particular pride in his "Sammlung von Werkzeugen der Naturlehre," which includes not only an "Elektrizitätsmesser," but also a barometer, a thermometer, and a "Luftblau- und Feuchtigkeitsmesser" (*NS* 102). The apparent motivation and justification for all this is the imperative of reason: the purpose of collecting is not just the mindless aggregation of objects or statistics, but the progression towards understanding and hence mastery implied in Stifter's trio of nouns "Beobachter, Klassifizierer, Kenner." To observe the world and thereby identify its patterns and processes offers the opportunity of mastering the threat posed by its potential uncontrollability. For example, by pressing and classifying moss or butterflies, as do the characters in "Der Kuß von Sentze" and "Der Waldgänger" respectively, it appears that man can organise nature into static categories according to which he can reasonably begin to comprehend it.

Central to the act of collecting, then, is the control that is achieved over the forces of nature. "Der Waldgänger" is revealing in this respect. Here, Georg neatly labels each of his stones ("auf jedem war ein kleines Zettelchen geklebt, welches den Namen des Minerales angab," *GW* III: 458). This detail is repeated in *Der Nachsommer*, in which Heinrich's initial collection consists of minerals stuck to pieces of card with their

names attached, thereby removed from their natural, wild context ("[Die Mineralien] waren schon Sammlungsstücke, hatten meistens das Papierstückchen mit ihrem Namen auf sich aufgeklebt," *NS* 27). We find a similar system of categorisation in the two collections of culti-vated garden roses which we encounter in this georgic novel. Risach, for example, recounts that when he saw the assemblage of roses at Mathilde's family home, he was struck by the realisation that: "Sie waren nach einem sinnvollen Plane geordnet, das zeigte sich gleich bei dem ersten Blicke. Alle Stämmchen trugen Täfelchen mit ihren Na-men" (*NS* 639). In later life, he himself observes the same orderly practice of attaching name-plates to the *Rosenhaus* roses (whilst also using a cage-like device to restrain their natural, proliferous tendencies, *NS* 42; the word "Gitter" is repeated seven times on this page).[6] Most importantly, however, this orderliness is not restricted to man's control over external nature. As is perhaps most evident in *Der Nachsommer* and *Witiko*, it is wedded to a belief in a whole life of moderation and *self*-control, as we see in the numerous references to "collecting one-self" or "collecting one's thoughts."[7]

But how is this orderliness upheld by the characters within the fic-tion? Again, *Der Nachsommer* is revealing in that order is maintained in both the Drendorf household and the *Rosenhaus* by unwritten rules: in the former, for example, the children are forbidden to enter their par-ents' bedroom, and the owner of the latter dictates that felt slippers must always be worn in order to prevent the marble floor from being damaged. In both dwellings, the rooms are allowed to be used only for their designated purpose. Likewise, the "Sitte" ("custom," *NS* 50) of placing books back on their shelves as soon as they have been inspected is closely adhered to by the occupants of both houses. This, according to Heinrich, conveys a sense of both "Ordnung und Reinheit" (*NS* 193), the latter word being another key term in Stifter's evocation of both his characters' collected lives and their physical collections. Their gardens reflect not only the possibility of categorising nature but also the need to eradicate the least sign of taint or blemish, as epitomised by Risach's insistence that his trees be systematically washed and scrubbed with a brush and soapy water (*NS* 131; similarly fastidious details recur elsewhere: in "Brigitta," the narrator is struck by the workers systemati-cally polishing each leaf of the camellias; in "Der Waldgänger," Georg's father cleans the stems of his rose bushes; in "Zwei Schwestern," even the narrator cleans and orders his tree trunks[8]). The word "rein" pre-dominates in Heinrich's description of the *Rosenhaus* roses: he sees them as "sehr rein" and "besonders rein und klar," a quality shared by those in the gardens of Mathilde's *Sternenhof*, which are "rein und

schön" (*NS* 41, 53, 261). Furthermore, their spotlessness is rendered even more pure and pristine by the systematic elimination of all the defects, such as insects, sickness, and natural decay, that one might normally expect to find in a rose bush (*NS* 41).

Such cleanliness, however, is confined neither to external nature nor to *Der Nachsommer*, but is found within the walls of nearly all Stifter's fictional houses. Ludmilla in "Der Hagestolz" is, tellingly, a washerwoman (as is the mother of Johanna in "Kalkstein"), and when we initially encounter her, she is standing on her tiptoes wiping away the dust from her already scrubbed furniture: "[sie war] damit beschäftigt . . . , von den weißgescheuerten Tischen, Stühlen und Schreinen den Staub abzuwischen, und die Dinge, die sich etwa gestern Abends verschoben hatten, wieder zu recht zu stellen." Her house accordingly bears not a blemish with its "glänzende Fenster," "ruhige weiße Vorhänge," and "reiner gebohnter Fußboden" (1,6: 20–2). The vicarage in "Der Waldgänger" is equally orderly and spotless: everywhere is "äußerst reinlich," and Georg's mother is dedicated to the pursuit of "Reinlichkeit" (*GW* III: 433–4). A similarly superlative cleanliness is observed in Mathilde Makloden's childhood home, where Risach notices that "Alles war auf das reinlichste geputzt" (*NS* 645). Such abstersive habits are equally observed by Heinrich's father, who insists on cleaning his own rooms, whose spotlessness causes Heinrich to comment: "Überhaupt durfte bei dem Vater kein Zimmer die Spuren des unmittelbaren Gebrauches zeigen, sondern mußte immer aufgeräumt sein" (*NS* 8).

Evidently, this urge to eradicate all trace of dirt or disorder is no gratuitous detail. What it would appear to indicate on the surface is a moral dimension to the "Sammelgeist," whereby the notion of "Reinheit" carries implications of spiritual purity as well as physical untouchedness and untouchability. In this sense, the word "Sitte" (*NS* 50) not only suggests the customary nature of Risach's actions, but also attributes a moral significance to them. Moreover, explicitly sacral images are invoked in the description of the roses and library in the *Rosenhaus*. Heinrich speaks of the library as a "temple" (*NS* 193) and compares rooms in which order does not prevail to "Kirchen, in denen man mit Trödel wirtschaftet" (*NS* 193), whilst Risach remembers the "temple of roses" in the Maklodens' garden (*NS* 639).

In *Der Nachsommer* the elements that constitute Stifter's putative weltanschauung really appear to coalesce in the form of the marble statue, arguably the centre-piece of all the fictive collections. A crucial reason for marble's desirability is its intrinsic purity, as Heinrich indicates when he first observes the statue: "Die Stirne war rein, und es ist begreiflich, daß man nur aus Marmor so etwas machen kann" (*NS*

326). The sacral quality of this purity is then emphasised in Heinrich's approving soliloquy: "Mir dünkte es gut, daß man diese Gestalt . . . in einen Raum getan hat, der ihr allein gehört, der sein Licht von oben bekömmt, und sie mit einer dämmerigen Helle wie mit einem Tempel umfängt" (NS 327). Moreover there is a moral significance to the marble, as Emil Merker (rightly) implies when he (wrongly) comments on Stifter's art as a whole: "Leidenschaften sind für Stifter Dämonen, die er aus dem weißmarmornen Tempel seiner Kunst ausschließt."[9] In this respect the statue is, of course, not solely representative of comfortable Biedermeier morality; it also refers back to the age of Graeco-Roman classical restraint and the kind of eternal, essential beauty enshrined in Homer's Nausicaa, of whom the marble form reminds Heinrich.[10] For this reason, Der Nachsommer appears at face value to constitute the pinnacle of Stifter's Apollonian art, providing surely the fullest demonstration of his noble vision of artistic beauty as a manifestation of the divine ("[die Kunst] war überall und ist überall die Darstellung des Göttlichen im Gewande des Reizes," GW VI: 260).

Even at just the surface level of Stifter's writings, however, collections do not simply provide the tangible expression of an unchanging moral beauty that transcends "täglicher Gebrauch" (NS 327): the physical objects that make up a collection also represent an attempt by Stifter to substantiate his professed belief in a divinely underwritten universe. This is most clearly demonstrated by the way in which "Dinge" ("things"), both natural and man-made, feature in Stifter's stories; and I shall examine their overt significance before turning to the more disturbing shapes which they may conceal.[11] Various critics have recognised the connection between Stifter's "things" and his notion of a God-given world. J. P. Stern, for instance, refers to "things" that have fulfilled their true value as "Stifter's Utopia"[12]; whilst Wilhelm Dehn is unequivocal in his claim that "Die Dinge sind in ihrer Gesamtheit ein Ausdruck des Göttlichen."[13] Likewise, Irmscher attributes intrinsic wholeness and immutable identity to Stifter's "things": "Jedes Ding hat seine von Ewigkeit her festgesetzte unverwechselbar eigene Struktur, durch die es seine Selbständigkeit in der Welt hat."[14] A crucial question is implicit here: to what extent can the universe be perceived in terms of divine essence? Stifter appears to harbour no doubts about his answer. He ascribes the wholeness of eternal meaning to "things," a meaning that is ultimately accessible to passion-riven man — and that Heinrich Drendorf and Witiko's Huldrik clearly long to grasp (Heinrich speaks of his desire to fathom "das Unnennbare, was in den Dingen vor mir lag," NS 293, and Huldrik claims: "Wir suchen die Dinge wahrzunehmen, wie es sein kann," 5,2: 289). Stifter constantly seeks to give the

impression that man is subordinate to the objects that make up the world around him, and that the relationship between the two consists in man listening to and obeying the higher voice of the "Dinge in ihrer objektiven Giltigkeit (nicht in einseitigen Beziehungen zu unsern Leidenschaften)" (*GW* VI: 7). This is made evident in "Der Kuß von Sentze" by the words that he attributes to the moss-collector Walchon: "Nur die Naturdinge sind ganz wahr. Um was man sie vernünftig fragt, das beantworten sie vernünftig" (*GW* III: 707). Of course, we can appreciate the meaning of "things" only through rigorous restraint of our passions, as Risach indicates: "wenn ein Übermaß von Wünschen und Begehrungen in uns ist, so hören wir nur diese immer an, und vermögen nicht die Unschuld der Dinge außer uns zu fassen" (*NS* 189). Later in the novel the same character provides us with a clarion example of the purported faith in the transcendent nature of "things" that lies at the heart of his own "Indian summer":

> Die Ehrfurcht vor den Dingen, wie sie an sich sind, war bei mir so groß, daß ich bei Verwicklungen streitigen Ansprüchen und bei der Notwendigkeit, manche Sachen zu ordnen, nicht auf unsern Nutzen sah, sondern auf das, was die Dinge nur für sich forderten, und was ihrer Wesenheit gemäß war, damit sie das wieder werden, was sie waren, und das, was ihnen genommen wurde, erhalten, ohne welchem sie nicht sein können, was sie sind. (*NS* 614)

The classical ideal of the unambiguous "Ding an sich" to which Risach refers is one which Stifter constantly seeks to maintain.[15] In "Der Waldgänger," for example, Georg is drawn to "Dinge, die schon an und für sich da sind" (*GW* III: 442). A similar ideal of essence in the Platonic sense may be detected in the repeated use of the typically Stifterian phrase "Wesenheit der Dinge" ("essence of things")[16] — a formulation that imputes a kind of "beingness" to physical objects (and a phrase that significantly becomes more and more frequent towards the end of the author's life).

Whilst maintaining the "objektive Giltigkeit" of physical things and stressing the subordinate role that man plays in relation to objects, Irmscher does nevertheless place them in a broader human context in his discussion of the "Sammelgeist."[17] Likewise, Martin and Erika Swales remark of Stifter: "objects . . . are for him, ideally, emblems of sound being. No one tried harder to give all things that human radiance and loveliness, that 'aura' of which Walter Benjamin spoke when he talked of the intimacy which ownership, collecting, involves."[18] Again, *Der Nachsommer* provides the reader with some of the most apparently unambiguous and idealistic statements about the spiritual value of collecting and the way in which it can be used to achieve man's positive

potential, his essentially "sound being." Risach, for example, states: "Was ich bedurfte, . . . fand ich in den Sammlungen" (*NS* 626); and Heinrich's father is quick to point out that his recognition of the intrinsic meaning of the objects in his collection has fostered his own growth:

> Diese Steine sind durch viele Jahre mein Vergnügen gewesen. Oft in trüben Stunden, wenn Sorgen und Zweifel das Leben seines Duftes beraubten, und es dürr vor mich hinzubreiten schienen, bin ich zu dieser Sammlung gegangen, habe diese Gestalten angeschaut, bin in eine andere Zeit und in eine andere Welt versetzt worden, und bin ein anderer Mensch geworden. (*NS* 400)

Like the marble, though, these objects fuse a kind of transcendent idealism with a sound moral. Not only is Herr Drendorf aware of the "Wesenheit der Dinge"; he also recognises the ethical influence that these "things" can exert over man, as we see from his comment: "wer in dem Besitze einer so trefflichen Sammlung der schönsten zahlreichen und dabei so mannigfaltigen Gegenstände ist, der kann niemals mehr bei seinen Anordnungen in das Unbedeutende Leere und Nichtige verfallen" (*NS* 374).

All in all, it may seem that Stifter offers an overwhelmingly positive appearance of wholeness; he appears to leave the reader with the sense that the universe is indeed cohesive and continuous. Not only do the individual objects in a collection make up what Heinrich perceives to be "ein Ganzes . . . , welches man nicht zerstückt denken konnte" (*NS* 285), but they are also in themselves whole, possessing an essence, a "Geist," that transcends the human limits of space and time as well as life and death, and that enshrines the past, present and future. The immortal value of objects for Stifter is made clear in the essay "Der Tandelmarkt" (The Flea Market, 1844), where he tries to convince us that even the most humble "Plunder und Trödel," the "ganz unnützes, mittelalterliches Zeugs," speaks to us of the "alltägliches Alltagsleben unserer Voreltern" (*MSB* 367–9). Similarly, Risach is made to argue that the "Geist der Traulichkeit und Innigkeit" that dwells in physical objects survives through the generations, so that their intrinsic meaning can still be apprehended in the present (*NS* 258). Furthermore, this meaning, so Stifter suggests through Risach, will last far beyond man's death in the form of the constantly developing body of scientific knowledge of which the process of collecting is the essential prerequisite:

> Ich glaube . . . , daß in der gegenwärtigen Zeit der Standpunkt der Wissenschaft, von welcher wir sprechen, der des Sammelns ist. Entfernte Zeiten werden aus dem Stoffe etwas bauen, das wir noch nicht kennen. Das Sammeln geht der Wissenschaft immer voraus; das ist

nicht merkwürdig; denn das Sammeln muß ja vor der Wissenschaft sein. (*NS* 110)

On the face of it, then, the collecting habits of Stifter's characters are rooted in reason, measure, and morality, and Eric Blackall might seem to be right when he confidently declares that there is "no sign of obsession . . . in Stifter's writings."[19] Man, it appears, can grasp the "essence of things" to which he is subordinate and use this insight to locate himself firmly within the solid foundations of the house of certainty and meaning. Yet on closer inspection it becomes clear that this house is poised on a substructure more precarious than we might initially imagine. The story "Prokopus" (Prokopus, 1848) is particularly revealing in this respect. The narrator does not deny that things have an essence; nor does he deny that humans have been given the power to fathom this. But who has given them this power? How exactly are they to use it? One day we may be able to answer such questions, but, if we ever can, it will be at some unimaginably remote point in the future, when humanity might no longer even exist ("nach Abschluß des Menschlichen," *NS* 388). In the meantime, no matter how much pain it may cause us, we must watch things unfold according to their own impenetrable logic: "Die natürlichen Dinge gehen ihren Lauf, wir mögen noch so großen Schmerz darüber empfinden" (*GW* III: 560). Moreover, that Stifter the man was himself not entirely convinced of the absolute value of his own energetically pursued collecting urge can be surmised from a letter of 7 December 1850 to Dr. Karl Donberger, in which he implicitly rejects the notion that collections are grounded in a satisfying faith in the intrinsic value of objects:

> Es ist fast ein lächerlicher Gedanke, daß ein ernsthafter deutscher Autor und Schulrat und ein ernsthafter deutscher Doktor der Medizin sich um ein dem Zerfalle entgegen gehendes deutsches Geräte im Ernste Mühe geben . . . ; aber es tut nichts, ich mache meiner Frau das Vergnügen . . . Nach unserem Tode wird bei unserer Lizitation ein schreckliches Gelächter sein. (*MSB* 705–6)

If we return to the texts, we find the same dual perspective given artistic expression. As I noted earlier, Stifter's delineation of collections appears grounded in the belief that objects can be categorised and controlled through the application of reason; and the primacy of reason appears to be implicit in the portrayal of his collectors' rooms and activities. This might seem to be exemplified in the story "Der Waldsteig." Tiburius, like the *Rentherr* in "Turmalin," apparently leads a stable, controlled life: he gathers together furniture, carpets, curtains, and clothes — all emblems implying solidity. Yet these same emblems

give rise to a feeling of excess, an impression of *too much* solidity: a sense that, for Stifter, extreme stability is in fact irredeemably linked with extreme instability.[20] Far from pointing to a fulfilled and fulfilling life, a profound precariousness pervades Tiburius's collection, indicating a fictive existence trembling between order and chaos. Although, as we would expect, the collection in the book version of "Der Waldsteig" appears to be more demonstrative of calm reflection than the collection in the journal version, it is in the later one that Stifter writes of Tiburius's objects: "Zur Unruhe mehrten sich viele Dinge" (1,6: 152). In this one significant sentence, which stands out through its very brevity, another perspective is at work: one which throws into question the whole notion that man is able rationally to control and categorise the accumulated matter external to him.

The same emblems in Tiburius's collection that connote the stability of reason thus point equally to its chaotic dysfunctionality. A comparison of the two versions of the story makes this particularly clear. In the journal version, for instance, it is stated rather casually of Tiburius: "Seine Pfeifensammlung war die schönste im Lande" (1,3: 114). The book version, in contrast, is more communicative: "Auch eine Pfeifensammlung hatte er, die später in schöne Schreine gethan werden sollte, jezt aber noch auf den Tischen lag" (1,6: 152). This increase in information, however, serves only to make the collection of pipes more disturbing. The emphasis of the description now lies on the disorder of this collection, which has outgrown the control of its instigator, which exhibits no clear pattern and performs no discernible function: like the stripes on the boy Tiburius's underwear, it is an accumulation of objects "alle außer dem Nuzen" (1,6: 147; no such line appears in the journal version). In this respect, Tiburius's collections resemble that of his fellow eccentric, the *Rentherr* in "Turmalin." Tiburius's bizarre collection of pictures of men's heads emerges again in the *Rentherr*'s apartment (and, interestingly, in a slightly different form in *Der Nachsommer*[21]), and the *Rentherr*'s unnamed and unnameable collection of bric-à-brac finds its analogue in Tiburius's functionless conglomeration of "viele Sachen" and "umliegende Geräthe"(1,6: 151, 183). It is hardly surprising to learn that the *Rentherr* lost his sanity and subsequently disappeared from ordinary society; indeed his disintegration, like Tiburius's, is latent in the rooms where he heaps up his possessions. Furthermore, it is no exaggeration to suggest that for Stifter's characters in general, collecting may be a pathological compulsion rather than a reasonable hobby, especially in the light of the extraordinary giveaway sentence concerning Tiburius's collecting mania that Stifter included in the journal version of "Der Waldsteig" (but characteristically excised in the

book version): "Endlich war er so schlecht geworden, daß er alle Symptome der Pathologie auf einmal an sich hatte" (1,3: 117).[22]

Far from upholding the ideology of reason, these fictive collections serve to throw it into question. The more the characters manically attempt to organise and list their collections, the more these objects not only resist categorisation, but wreak a kind of revenge on humans. That people gradually but inexorably become submerged by an imbroglio of irrational objects they cannot control is evident even in "Der Tandelmarkt," where Stifter says of a man he once knew (and who could quite easily be substituted for the *Rentherr* or Tiburius): "In diesem Hause nun saß der Mann, umringt mit Dingen seiner Ururgroßväter" (*MSB* 370).[23] We are left with the sense that Stifter's characters seek *too* strongly to avouch the potency of the "Licht [der] Vernunft" (2,2: 135), and that Stifter himself so deeply feared the inadequacy of human reason that he obsessively sought to provide proofs of its power and dependability.

I have suggested that for Stifter, man's intellect may be incapable of fathoming the chaos of objects exterior to him; that he is surrounded by possessions which are poised between orderliness and disarray. However, the texts by no means solely demonstrate this threatening collapse of reason. A closer inspection suggests that behind the facade of these external items, there lurks a hidden subtext which relates to inner man: that a chaos similar to the one I have identified in external objects lies beneath the orderly mask which the humans who collect them present to the world. That articles are not objectively gathered for their intrinsic value is made clear in *Der Nachsommer*, where, despite his protestations about the qualities inherent in marble, Risach refuses to include any pieces in his collection that he personally has not found (*NS* 202–5); behaviour that again has all the characteristics of a compulsion:

> Ich habe meine Marmore alle selber in den Gebirgen gesammelt, und habe ihren Bruch aus den Felsen ihr Absägen ihr Schleifen und ihre Einfügungen geleitet. Die Arbeit hat mir manche Freude gebracht, und ich glaube, daß mir nur darum diese Steine so lieb sind, weil ich sie selber gesucht habe . . . Da ich allen Marmor selber gesammelt habe, so kann ich wohl auch kein Stück an meinem Hause anbringen, das mir von fremder Hand käme. (*NS* 111)

This is not the collection of "Dinge, wie sie an sich sind" that Risach professes it to be towards the end of the novel (*NS* 614): it appears in the novel to reveal covertly the obsessive nature of the hoarder. In this respect, it is illuminating to consider the treatment of cacti in both Stifter's life and his oeuvre, for here we see that objectivity is not his prime concern: objects capture him solely for the way in which they

relate to man. Fischer was one of the first critics to probe Stifter's "cactus fetish,"[24] and he convincingly argues that the author's excessive fondness for these plants does not show him to be a "biedermeierlicher Biedermann."[25] On the contrary: "die Schablonen seiner Zeit dienen ihm als Maskerade, aber nicht als Selbstzweck. Er geht in seinen Liebhabereien nicht auf, beglückt und weltbefriedet, sondern er verbirgt sich hinter ihnen . . . die Pflanzen treten an die Stelle mitmenschlicher Kommunikation."[26] Fischer's argument is corroborated by a revealing letter to Heckenast of 24 May 1857, in which Stifter writes:

> Was Sie von Senkes Cacteenanstalt schrieben, hat mich sehr in Anspruch genommen, die Pflege dieser merkwürdigen Gewächse hat für mich in meiner Einsamkeit etwas Reizendes und Seelenerfüllendes, da mir das Gedeihen und wundervolle Blühen dieser Gewächse den Umgang mit Menschen ersetzt. (*MSB* 752)

Significantly, this letter was written whilst Stifter was putting the finishing touches to *Der Nachsommer*, a novel in which, as I have mentioned, the *Cereus Peruvianus* receives constant attention. With both Fischer's and Stifter's declarations in mind, it seems fair to suggest that Stifter dwells obsessively on this rare cactus not for its botanical specificity (nor even solely for the control that man exercises over nature in tending it), but because of its hidden connection with Heinrich's inner development — and, specifically, with his *sexual* maturity. For example, it is on his and Natalie's wedding day — the day on which, so one would assume, they consummate their relationship — that we finally witness the once-in-a-lifetime flowering of the *Cereus*'s "fabelhafte weiße Blumen" (*NS* 532).[27] Clearly, Stifter is obliquely alluding here to that very thing he apparently considered too odious to mention: human sexuality. Moreover, the interest he displays is scarcely mild or moderate: the *manic* focus on the cactus suggests that he finds this very human concern fascinating beyond all measure. Thus we find that it is partly *sexual* energy that impels the characters to frantic bouts of sublimational collecting; this desire to accumulate objects is essentially a "Drang" (*NS* 110), an uncontrollable impulse. We even find a direct link between erotic urges and the urge to collect specifically implied by Stifter himself in one of his more unusual uses of the word "sammeln." In a line which is unsurprisingly not retained in the book version of "Brigitta," the Major says: "ich darf keinen Sohn haben, ich weiß nicht, wie seine Liebe thut, ich muß mir fremde sammeln — —" (1,2: 229), thereby, we presume, alluding to his multitude of sexual conquests.

It is instructive here to look more precisely at the objects that the characters so avidly collect. As Watanabe-O'Kelly rightly points out in an essay with the telling subtitle "Sexuelle Erziehung eines Narren,"

Stifter makes a clear link in "Der Waldsteig" between Tiburius's collections and his sexual development — or lack of it.[28] Although Watanabe-O'Kelly provides a full and persuasive interpretation of the story, a couple of points may be added to her argument to illuminate the relationship between sexual energy and collecting still further. Although the book version is less forthcoming than the journal version in divulging the explicit details of Tiburius's relationships, it is nonetheless the later version that provides the reader with the clearer link between Tiburius's collection and his refusal to marry. The narrator of the journal version merely reports: "Als die Erzieher wegfielen, . . . wollten ihn alle Mädchen heiraten, aber sie waren ihm nur abgeschmackt. Er schaffte alles an, was man gewöhnlich von dem Reichthume fordert" (1,3: 114). In the book version, however, the character's fictive psychology is more clearly defined. The narrator implies that Tiburius accumulates objects as a sublimation of the urges blocked off by his fear of women — in other words, that his collecting mania is generated by a sexual impetus: "es [gab] sehr viele Mädchen, welche den Herrn Tiburius geheirathet hätten, er erfuhr es auch immer, aber er fürchtete sich, und that es durchaus nicht. Er fing im Gegentheile an, für sich seinen Reichthum zu genießen" (1,6: 151). Moreover, the increasing abnormality of his actions in the book version is subtly highlighted by the small but significant omission of the word "gewöhnlich" from this version.

Thus far, I have regarded only the objects in Tiburius's house. However, of equal significance is another of his hobbies, namely art. For one thing, his drawings themselves are, to say the least, unusual, and they confirm his reputation as a crank when an entire sketchbook proves to contain nothing but endless repetitions of the same chiaroscuro theme ("man [entdekte] darin die Seltsamkeit . . . , daß er ganz und gar lauter Helldunkel zeichne," 1,6: 187). Quite apart from the subject-matter, the very fact that he works so obsessively suggests that the forces underlying his collecting mania also compel him to create the same picture over and over again. In this context it is eloquent that he stops painting once he has met Maria. The notion of art as a frantic sublimational activity is intimated even more clearly in the later story "Nachkommenschaften" (Descendants, 1864). The narrator defines himself as a landscape painter at the very outset ("So bin ich unversehens ein Landschaftsmaler geworden. Es ist entsetzlich," *GW* III: 565) and, shortly afterwards, he hints that his painting absolves him altogether from sexual urges ("Ich werde . . . gar niemals ein Weib bekommen, weil mir an einem solchen gar nichts liegt," *GW* III: 571). His unwillingness to reveal his pictures, moreover, suggests that on one

level he himself is half-aware of his own inner processes: he even ventures out to Lüpfing to purchase extra locks for his rooms so that no one can see the paintings, and he most pointedly refuses to show the beautiful Susanna his hurriedly hidden canvas when they first meet (*GW* III: 583). That it is essentially a sexual dynamic driving him to paint is even more strongly suggested by the way in which his relationship with Susanna develops. He initially chances upon her in the forest, but then makes a daily habit of these brief encounters. During this period, he still paints ("Sobald es das Licht erlaubte, war ich schon an meiner Malerei") — but as soon as he sees Susanna's carriage approaching, he casts his paintbrush aside and rushes out into the forest ("so warf ich Pinsel und Malerbrett weg . . . , und begegnete ihr auf dem Waldwege," *GW* III: 616). After his and Susanna's love-declaration, however, he stops painting altogether ("ich [malte] nicht mehr," *GW* III: 624); the closer they become, the more pictures he shows her (*GW* III: 632); and just before they marry he frantically burns not only his *chef d'oeuvre* but also his preliminary studies, paints, paintbrushes and boards (*GW* III: 636). The intimate relationship between the compulsion to paint and other powerful forces within the narrator is, furthermore, implied by his acquaintance Peter Roderer in a typically ambiguous remark: "Sie haben sich der Landschaftsmalerei ergeben nicht des Geldes wegen, nicht des Ruhmes wegen, nicht aus Eitelkeit . . . , sondern Sie . . . wollen die Tiefe erschöpfen" (*GW* III: 591). That a sexual dynamic may even lie at the heart of *all* creative activity is, moreover, slyly betrayed by a tiny remark made by Risach in *Der Nachsommer*, who speaks of "Schaffungslust" as a "Trieb" (*NS* 612).

These are the same underlying "Triebe" that generate Tiburius's compulsion to collect strawberries after encountering Maria in the forest in "Der Waldsteig." Again, the book version is more suggestive than its predecessor. After having known Maria for only a short while, Tiburius addresses her in the journal version as "theuerster, liebster Engel" (1,3: 135), thus making his feelings for her quite obvious. These words are omitted from the book version, in which the couple's relationship develops much more gradually and is evoked indirectly on the whole, through the symbols of the basket and the strawberries that they collect together. It is worth noting in this respect that the words "sammeln" and "gesammelt" occur in the context of their relationship seven times in five pages (1,6: 195–200), as opposed to once in the journal version (1,3: 134). Even more significantly, Tiburius feels both "Verlangen" and "Hunger" (1,6: 188) after catching a glimpse of the ripe strawberries under the white cloth in the book version, words with clear sexual connotations. Sure enough, he goes on to become fixated on

both the fruit, which he fervently starts to collect, and the basket with its white cloth cover. Here, of course, we find an unmistakable parallel with "Kalkstein." Johanna, too, carries a basket covered with white cloth that barely conceals the spotless underwear inside.[29] When the girl's mother forces the couple to part, the priest-to-be begins his own dubious collection of exquisite linen, his passion undiminished, which leaves us in little doubt that this is no normal undertaking but an irrepressible compulsion. In his seminal article on "Kalkstein," Reddick convincingly refers to the priest's "Wäschemanie"[30] or, still more pertinently, his "radikaler Sammeltrieb,"[31] stressing with his use of the word "Trieb" the unspoken sexual dynamic driving the priest's obsession with the linen as well as his equally suspect obsession with hoarding money.

Clearly, the underlying threat in Stifter's texts does not reside only in the external world of objects that potentially defy man's reason. It lies to a perhaps even greater extent inside man, the objects in the collections frequently signifying his tumultuous sexual passions. Put very simply, collecting seems to provide a rampart against the chaos of human voluptuousness. Being so compulsive, however, it betrays its sexual origins, and it thereby provides Stifter and his characters with the ideal opportunity imperceptibly but incessantly to focus on their true obsession, human passion. The collection of roses in *Der Nachsommer* shows the same force at work in the characters' attempts to collect and control nature. I pointed out earlier that Risach's roses exude an air of praiseworthy order. Alexander Stillmark would seem to agree with this: he sees the rose-growing as "a willing sacrifice" and a reflection of the "chastening process of moral growth."[32] But he does not acknowledge that in its very excess this orderliness in fact comes across as subtly menacing — and, furthermore, as an obsessive attempt to control *human* nature. The works convey an increasing mania for trimming, training and controlling nature's inherent rampancy as it becomes in *human* eyes ever more symbolic of *human* tendencies that, for Stifter, mean disaster. Risach grows the roses wholly and solely as a reminder of the inordinate passion he felt for Mathilde, and he obsessively orders and lists them in accordance with his enforced renunciation of her. By putting them all behind bars (the "Gitter" he erects on every hand), he not only ensures the contained and orderly growth of the plants, but in symbolic terms also maintains his own upright conduct, preventing the passion that has been suppressed but not eradicated from running riot again. Tellingly, the word "Trieb" (meaning both "plant shoots" and "primitive urges") is actually used in *Der Nachsommer*, specifically in the context of controlling nature:

> Wie überhaupt der Mensch einen Trieb hat, die Natur zu besiegen,
> und sich zu ihrem Herrn zu machen, . . . so sucht auch der Bergbe-
> wohner seine Berge, die er lieb hat, zu zähmen. (NS 422)

The tendency towards categorisation embodied in Stifter's characters thus not only reflects man's ability or inability rationally to fathom
nature at large; it is equally concerned with man's ability or inability to
tame *human* nature or, more specifically, overwhelmingly human sexual
desires. This is one of the subtexts that Michael Kaiser recognises in his
interpretation of the ritual actions in "Der Kuß von Sentze" when he
states: "das Sammeln Walchons . . . schließlich gemahnt an gewisse
zwangsneurotische Verhaltensweisen."[33] Although Kaiser takes a dog-
matically Freudian line of argument, the link — implicit in the term
"Zwangsneurose" — that he makes between collecting (and similar ritual behaviours) and suppressed sexuality is nonetheless demonstrated
time and time again by Stifter's texts.[34] In order fully to appreciate this
relationship between Walchon's collection of moss and his own nature,
it is helpful to look at the hidden forces behind the other rites in "Der
Kuß von Sentze." The most obvious ritual is the one which gives the
story its title, namely that of kissing. Here, kisses are neatly organised
according to family tradition into two categories: "kiss of love," and
"kiss of peace" (GW III: 685). The minimalist action of the story concerns the elaborate preparations for the formal "kiss of peace" between
Rupert and Hiltiburg, preparations which Walchon outlines in pains-
taking detail for his nephew:

> Du weißt, daß diese Vorbereitungen darin bestehen, daß man drei
> Tage mit einem Gebete, mit Betrachtungen über den Schwur und mit
> Lesung der Schwurschriften hinbringe. Hiltiburg wird an dem nämli-
> chen Tage die Vorbereitungen antreten. Ich habe von den vorhan-
> denen Schwurschriften zwei Abschriften in dem Hause. Eine werde
> ich dir, eine Hiltiburg geben. Und am Morgen nach dem dritten
> Tage leistet ihr in dem Saale, ohne einen einzigen Zeugen als Gott,
> wie es vorgeschrieben ist, das Versprechen. (GW III: 710)

His inordinate insistence on this formula immediately raises the question: why should such ceremony be attached to one kiss? One reason
has to be that it is a way in which both Stifter and the characters can
attempt to restrict and define sexuality. The kiss is quite openly used as
a defence against sexual rivalry in the episode that is said to have taken
place between Rupert's father and Walchon. Both men once desired the
same woman, but both renounced her after exchanging a "kiss of
peace," the alleged — though highly implausible — result of which was
that both men put a stop to their lustful desires ("seit wir uns den Frie-
denskuß gegeben und ihn so gehalten habe, daß keiner mehr das

schöne Fräulein begehrte . . . ist oft der gleiche Spruch über unsere Lippen gegangen," *GW* III: 687). With this in mind, the subtext of Walchon's moss collection becomes more evident. This he initiates after renouncing the young beauty, again implying that his sexual desires are forced beneath the surface rather than extinguished, and that their suppression is reflected in his ritualistic pressing and desiccation of nature. The behaviour of the priest in "Kalkstein" is equally governed by his bottled up sexual desires, and he displays a similar tendency towards ritual behaviour when he places his linen in a special casket. Likewise, Tiburius and Maria treat the strawberries with elaborate ceremony before they are able to express themselves sexually to one another. Such acts are quite clearly symbolic: despite Stifter's and his characters' best efforts, sexuality is unremittingly sublimated into the obsessive rituals which are part of the fiction's unique appeal.

Notes

[1] Interestingly, Stifter also refers to *Bunte Steine* as a "collection" (2,2: 12).

[2] For a basic but useful discussion of the cultivation of nature in the Austro-Hungarian Empire of the mid-nineteenth century, see "Der kultivierende Blick: Die Welt als Garten," in *Adalbert Stifter: Schrecklich schöne Welt*, ed. Lachinger and Sturm, *VASILO* 39 (1990) 1/2: 86–91.

[3] Ferdinand van Ingen argues that such characters collect plants and observe the stars in order to understand the secrets of God-given nature ("Band und Kette: Zu einer Denkfigur bei Stifter," in *Adalbert Stifter: Dichter und Maler, Denkmalpfleger und Schulmann: Neue Zugänge zu seinem Werk*, ed. Laufhütte and Möseneder, [Tübingen: Niemeyer, 1996], 63). This is a prime example of the way in which even recent criticism does not necessarily probe beneath the texts' surfaces.

[4] Walter Höllerer, "Stifter," in Walter Höllerer, *Zwischen Klassik und Moderne: Lachen und Weinen in der Dichtung einer Übergangszeit* (Stuttgart: Klett, 1958), 373.

[5] This is elaborated upon in the ensuing pages, with references to "Raritätensammlungen" and "Meteorsammlungen" (*MSB* 408). Moreover, Stifter uses the word "sammeln" to speak of his interest in entomology, antiquities and meteorology: "Ich war eigentlich seit meinen Studien her ein Grübler . . . , vorzugsweise aber beschäftigte ich mich mit Sammlungen von Käfern und Altertümern, an Wettersammeln dachte ich nicht, ich meinte auch, es gäbe kein solches Ding" (*MSB* 407).

[6] The word "Gitter" is repeated in various forms and to striking effect when Heinrich first stumbles across the *Rosenhaus* (thirteen times in sixteen pages).

"Gitter" in their many forms are one of the most fascinating images in Stifter's evocations of physical/symbolic space. The Major in "Brigitta," for instance, has an unscalable wall around his house, and the word "Gitter" is reiterated in the context of his dwelling with astonishing frequency (seven times in three pages: 1,5: 422–4). "Gitter" are also used to telling effect in "Kalkstein" (see 2,2: 112–15; all in the context of Johanna); "Turmalin" (2,2: 135, 145); and "Bergmilch" (Mountain Quartz, 1853; 2,2: 320, 338, 351). Do we suppose that the protagonists erect them in order to prevent intruders from getting in? Or are we to suppose that they act as a restraint on the characters' own inner selves? It is fascinating in this respect that so many of the characters/narrators lock their bedroom doors on the inside, even when their hosts have stopped locking them in from the outside.

[7] See, for example, 5,1: 160. For a more unusual use of the idiom, see 5,1: 235.

[8] 1,5: 432, *GW* III: 438, 1,6: 271.

[9] Emil Merker, "Nachwort" to "Der Hochwald" (Stuttgart: Reclam, 1988), 127–8.

[10] The classical aspect of the statue is, furthermore, suggested by Heinrich's comment: "Ich sah die Überreste einer alten untergegangenen Welt in den Marmoren, die in dem Gebirge vorkommen" (*NS* 34).

[11] For the most fascinating and thorough study of the role of "things" in Stifter's work, see Wilhelm Dehn, *Ding und Vernunft: Zur Interpretation von Stifters Dichtung* (Bonn: Bouvier, 1969).

[12] J. P. Stern, *Reinterpretations: Seven Studies in Nineteenth Century German Literature* (London: Thames and Hudson, 1964), 296.

[13] Dehn, *Ding und Vernunft*, 62.

[14] Hans Dietrich Irmscher, *Adalbert Stifter: Wirklichkeitserfahrung und gegenständliche Darstellung* (Munich: Fink, 1971), 104.

[15] Although Stifter uses the Kantian term "thing in itself" ("das Ding an sich"), his understanding of "things" differs from Kant's. Whereas Kant argued that the "thing in itself" certainly exists but is by definition not capable of being perceived because it is not accessible to our experience, Stifter claims (on the surface, at least) that humans *have* been given the faculties to perceive it. There is, in fact, no evidence to show that Stifter had Kant specifically in mind when he referred to "die Dinge." Obviously he, like all his contemporaries, was affected by Kant's thought. However, as the *Kommentar* to *Bunte Steine* suggests, Stifter probably had only second-hand knowledge of Kant, gained from the text books he read at Kremsmünster (2,3: 91). Dehn makes a similar point (see *Ding und Vernunft*, 5–6). See also 2,3: 91, and 2,3: 115 for other echoes of Kantian thought in *Bunte Steine*.

[16] See, for example, *NS* 292, 614, 719; *GW* III: 560, 726.

[17] Irmscher argues that one of the central themes of the book version of "Die Mappe" is the relationship between man and his past (Irmscher, *Wirklichkeitserfahrung und gegenständliche Darstellung*, 129).

[18] Swales and Swales, *Adalbert Stifter*, 38.

[19] Eric A. Blackall, *Adalbert Stifter: A Critical Study* (Cambridge: Cambridge UP, 1948). His full comment reads: "There is nothing pathological about control . . . There was nothing pathological about Stifter, nothing unusual about his mind — except that it was that of a great artist. There is no sign of obsession or hallucination in any of Stifter's writings . . . *Witiko* is a masterpiece of coherence . . . Even more striking is the extreme serenity which radiates from the new *Mappe meines Urgroßvaters*" (61).

[20] It is this kind of disturbance that Thomas Mann perceives when he suggests that things seem not to be quite right in "Der Hagestolz" (Mann, *Briefe*, 59).

[21] See *NS* 412.

[22] "Pathology" is a feature that Thomas Mann also perceives in Stifter's oeuvre. He writes: "Aber was für ein aufregender, außerordentlicher, alle Augenblicke ins Extreme, man kann schon sagen: Pathologische vorstoßender Erzähler der Mann außerdem und trotzdem ist" (Mann, *Briefe*, 458). Matz also recognises the "pathological" dimension, particularly in the case of "Der Waldgänger." He writes: "Die große Schönheit der Novelle, die klassische Vollkommenheit ihrer Sprache lassen leicht übersehen, wie dicht Stifter mit ihr an die Grenze des Pathologischen gewagt hat" (*Adalbert Stifter*, 249).

[23] A similar description of Tiburius is found in the book version of "Der Waldsteig": "So lebte Herr Tiburius unter allen diesen Dingen eine Weile fort" (1,6: 151).

[24] Kurt Gerhard Fischer, "Adalbert Stifter: Psychologische Beiträge zur Biographie," *VASILO*, 10 (1961): 85.

[25] Fischer, "Psychologische Beiträge," 70.

[26] Fischer, "Psychologische Beiträge," 70. Matz perceives a similar subtext. He asserts that Stifter lavished his attention on his cacti and dogs because they offered an outlet for those feelings of warmth and fondness which he could not give to or receive from the people in his life — not least his wife (*Adalbert Stifter*, 317).

[27] For a discussion of this plant in *Der Nachsommer*, see Martin Selge, "Stifters Kaktus: Zur naturwissenschaftlichen, (sexuel-)symbolischen und ästhetischen Dimension des *Cereus Peruvianus* in *Der Nachsommer*," in *Stifter Symposion: Vorträge und Lesungen*, ed. Lachinger (Linz, 1978), 28–37.

[28] For a penetrating analysis of "Der Waldsteig," see Helen Watanabe-O'Kelly, "Stifters *Der Waldsteig*: Sexuelle Erziehung eines Narren," in

Adalbert Stifter heute, 121–34. For her treatment of the collecting motif in particular, see 122.

[29] In both cases, the sexual symbolism of the basket is unmistakable.

[30] John Reddick, "Tiger und Tugend in Stifters *Kalkstein*: Eine Polemik," *Zeitschrift für deutsche Philologie*, 95 (1976): 246. Reddick convincingly associates the linen with the priest's fixation on Johanna. Alfred Winterstein, however, argues that the linen shows that the priest is in fact a secret transvestite; he offers further evidence for his theory when he remarks that priests wear dresses (*Adalbert Stifter: Persönlichkeit und Werk. Eine tiefenpsychologische Studie* [Vienna: Phönix, 1946], 186–7). What is particularly striking about this — apart from its implausibility — is that Winterstein more or less overlooks the Johanna episode: he refers to the priest as a "phallic woman" (186) and concentrates on his "feminine" attitude to his father (187). This formulaic Freudianism is matched in reductiveness only by commentators such as Margaret Gump who, astonishingly, sees no symbolism whatsoever in "Kalkstein." According to her, the priest could have solved all his problems by simply moving elsewhere: her comment that "he could probably have gotten a transfer to a better parish" is one of the most deliciously vacuous to be found in Stifter criticism (*Adalbert Stifter* [New York: Twayne, 1974], 80).

[31] Reddick, "Tiger und Tugend," 245. Winterstein also refers to the "Sammeltrieb" — but he refers only to Stifter's own collecting mania (*Adalbert Stifter: Persönlichkeit und Werk*, 22). He goes on to relate this wholly and solely to (Freudian) anal retentiveness: collecting is apparently a sublimation of Stifter's infantile desire to withhold his faeces (23). He pursues his argument to even more dismal extremes when he claims that all collectors are "Analerotiker," and that the objects they collect — quite regardless of their value or otherwise — are all "symbols of excrement" (23).

[32] Alexander Stillmark, "Stifter's Symbolism of Beauty: The Significance of the Flower in his Works," *Oxford German Studies*, 6 (1972): 87.

[33] Michael Kaiser, *Adalbert Stifter: Eine literaturpsychologische Untersuchung seiner Erzählungen* (Bonn: Bouvier, 1971), 107.

[34] Again, the vocabulary used has undeniably sexual connotations. For example, the desire to change the position of the easel is termed a "Drang" (*NS* 348), and the verb used in the same context is "treiben" (*NS* 348).

2: Masking the Void

"Das Unbedeutende Leere und Nichtige"
(*Der Nachsommer*)

AS WILL BE CLEAR FROM ALL THE STORIES discussed so far, collecting is by no means the only activity of Stifter's characters that displays the characteristics of a frenzied rite: it frequently goes hand in hand with a mania for cleanliness that goes far beyond ordinary domestic practicalities, exhibiting instead all the signs of an obsessive ritual. I noted earlier that this motif possesses an ethical dimension, but we can now identify a deeper and darker level. On this level Stifter's manic insistence on words such as "Maß," "Reinheit," and "Ordnung" suggests that the very opposite is the true focus of his works: that "Unmaß" and the dirt and disorder of unbridled sexuality are what fascinate him beyond measure. Schumacher for one recognises hidden depths to the "Mann eines strengsten Maßes."[1] Of Stifter's protestations of love for his wife Amalia (with whom he had a notoriously unhappy relationship), he asserts: "die ständigen Beteuerungen seiner Liebe tragen . . . den Stempel des Maßlosen."[2] Wolfgang Matz perceives similar subtexts: he argues that the emphasis on "Unschuld und Reinheit" in the fiction is "geradezu zwanghaft."[3] Rudolf Wildbolz, for his part, concentrates on what he calls "das zunehmende, geradezu rituelle Ernstnehmen" of the recurrent motifs of cleanliness and order.[4] As he rightly points out, "das Reinliche" in both Stifter's life and works is clearly an ambiguous area for, in protesting its validity, "[Stifter] tut es nicht als einer, dem all dies selbstverständlich und ruhig zu eigen ist: er tut es als einer, dem es zuinnerst fehlt."[5] It is clear that it is again the *excess* of cleanliness that Wildbolz finds disturbing when he states: "Das Viel dünkt uns ein Zuviel, es dünkt uns wunderlich, verdächtig, vermutlich auf ein Tieferes weisend."[6]

This suspect superabundance of ritual cleaning characterises both "Brigitta" and *Der Nachsommer*, stories with sexual passion at their hidden core. With the sexual subtext in mind, the characters' feverish scrubbing away at the leaves of their plants with soap and water can be read as a symbolic attempt to scour away the supposed filth of their own guilty passions — and one that simultaneously reveals these passions through the very excess of energy put into removing the slightest

stain. The depiction of Georg's mother in "Der Waldgänger" strongly
implies that the fixation on cleanliness and order is obsessive: she pursues "Reinlichkeit" to the exclusion of all other activities, and there is
surely an edge to the narrator's remark that she is so coruscating in her
crusade that the dust is fair driven away ("Sie . . . drang wie ein Son-
nenstrahl in alle Klüfte, daß der Staub sich entferne," *GW* III: 434).
His subsequent assertion that she serves as a paragon of moderation
("sie [gab] . . . das Beispiel . . . der sanftmütigen Mäßigung," *GW* III:
434) is a wonderfully Stifterian partial truth, for the appearance of
moderation is achieved only by obsessively immoderate means. The figure of Corona in the same story suggests the specifically sexual dimension partly through colour symbolism. Her house is a "Tempel der
Reinlichkeit" (*GW* III: 462), it is "unbedingt rein und klar und . . .
ordnungsgemäß" (*GW* III: 472), everything in it is laundered, painted,
scrubbed as white as white can be ("weiße Vorhänge," "schneeweiße
Linnen," "die Wände waren neu geweißt worden," "schneeweiß ge-
scheuerte Gefäße," *GW* III: 462) — but its roof is stridently *red* (*GW*
III: 469), a colour with obvious connotations. The same could be
averred in the case of Ludmilla in "Der Hagestolz" where, despite the
narrator's insistent use of the words "rein" and "weiß" (1,6: 20), we are
told that "Auf jeder der Wangen saß ein kleines, feines Flekchen Roth"
(1,6: 21). This fleeting hint of red slyly alludes to the sexual turmoil of
her younger days and brings to the apparent idyll an added dimension
that suggests that the strenuous purity of the scene is not quite as unproblematic as it may appear.[7] From this perspective, it seems clear that
in battling so vigorously against even the slightest manifestation of dirt
and disorder in her household, she is in truth keeping her own passion
in check. That the resultant spotlessness diverges from the norm is,
furthermore, openly indicated by the narrator's description of Ludmilla's house as "over-clean" ("[Victor] zog sich dann so zusammen
stimmend und passend an, wie er es in dem überreinlichen Hause seiner
Ziehmutter gelernt hatte," 1,6: 85). This pattern finds a clear and
equally telling parallel in "Kalkstein." Here, the protagonist has em-
braced a calling whose very task it is to be a model of cleanliness and
order ("andern als Muster der Reinlichkeit und Ordnung vorzuleuch-
ten," 2,2: 70); but of course he takes his pursuit of cleanliness far beyond the call of duty, to the point that the narrator describes him as
"beinahe ängstlich reinlich" (2,2: 70), plainly suggesting that his behaviour may be driven by neurosis. Interestingly, these words are an almost verbatim repetition of those that the narrator of "Feldblumen"
(Flowers of the Field, 1844) uses to evoke "Tusculum," the Utopia
from which raw passion ("jede rohe Leidenschaft," 1,4: 71) is entirely

banished: "Am Hause rückwärts bilden zwei Flügel einen Hof mit . . . Zimmern für die Thiere, die fast ängstlich rein gehalten werden" (1,4: 70–1). I have already argued that the priest's collection of fine linen in "Kalkstein" is motivated by his unabated passion. However, the linen is significant not only because the man so fervently collects it, but also because it reveals his mania for whiteness, the traditional emblem of purity. This is arguably the most insidious collection that Stifter ever created, for it denotes the priest's lily-white probity but at the same time expresses his undiminished and guilty fixation on the most intimate secrets of the washerwoman's young daughter. The significance of the linen has already been expounded in detail by Reddick,[8] but for these present purposes it suffices to suggest that the crucial issue is one of filth and purity. The two may seem to be opposites, but in this context are nothing more than two sides of the same coin: human sexuality. An obsessive cleansing ritual may be part of a frantic attempt to assert moral purity but, by its very obsessiveness, it betrays its source in turbid passion that may perhaps be contained but never eradicated.

We find a revealing parallel in *Der Nachsommer*, where even the marble, which appears to be the ultimate signifier of ethical purity, is irremediably linked with sexuality. Again and again we are told that it is free of taint and stain, as when it is described as "der Stoff . . . , der keine Makel hat" (*NS* 483), or when it is said to be "gar so schön und fast fleckenlos" (*NS* 370). However, it is significant that the focal point of the *Rosenhaus* is a marble statue of a woman; it is as if Stifter were trying to freeze fluid passion into something safe, something controllable. However, by dwelling so obsessively on the graven woman's white immaculacy (or *near* immaculacy: "*fast* fleckenlos"), Stifter brings to the marble subtle undertones of the sexual defilement that quietly but constantly threatens the *Rosenhaus*. It is interesting to note that this vision echoes one in "Feldblumen," written more than fifteen years earlier, where Albrecht sees a woman more beautiful and immaculate than any he has previously encountered, and instantly compares her with a walking Greek statue ("so müßte ein altgriechisches Marmorbild ausgesehen haben, das wandeln könnte und Augen gehabt hätte," 1,4: 55). Later, however, he suggests that this purity is in fact intrinsically stained: "es gibt einen größern Schmerz, den Schmerz verlorner Seelen, und der meine wäre derselbe, wenn ich sie auch nur bloß gekannt hätte, etwa als Mutter, Gattin — und dann den widrigen Flecken an dem Wunderwerke gesehen hätte" (1,4: 134–5). The many rules designed to maintain order in *Der Nachsommer* (that each room must be used for one purpose only; that felt shoes must be worn on the marble floors;

and that Heinrich's father sedulously cleans his own rooms) guard —
excessively — against this same threat of defilement.

It might be easy at this point to assume that the passion compelling
the characters to undertake such rituals is unequivocally condemned.
This, though, is not the case. Even on the surface of "Der Hochwald,"
for instance, Gregor — himself an embodiment of the values trumpeted
in the *Bunte Steine* preface — comforts Johanna by telling her that passion is wholly natural and the will of God (1,4: 290). In the preface,
Stifter advocates stringent self-restraint ("Bezwingung seiner selbst") as
a supposedly gentle virtue, to be achieved by all decent, ordinary folk
(2,2: 12). However, the very term "Bezwingung" itself is just as para-
doxical and problematic as the passion which it is supposed to restrain.
Far from being "gentle," it entails force: this unnatural "Zwang" para-
doxically *needs* passion in order to control passion; a condition of gen-
tleness is achieved only through turbulent struggle. Stifter's stories may
indeed be full of ordinary people with ordinary passions, but their protagonists are always *extra*-ordinary people with *extra*-ordinary passions:
"Charaktere . . . , die . . . weit über das Maß des Tages [hinausragen]"
(1,2: 238). Such people can control their inner tiger (to borrow
Stifter's own compelling image[9]) *only* by this process of relentless self-
restraint — and whilst this may be regarded as virtuous containment, it
may equally be regarded as appalling self-repression. Viewed in this latter way, there is a sense in which the diktat of order and decorum in
Der Nachsommer becomes an inhumane restriction on natural vitality,
maintained only "mit Zwang" (*NS* 125). Herr Drendorf's house, for
instance, is so obsessively orderly that it implies those "signs of pathology" explicitly identified in the journal version of "Der Waldsteig" (1,3:
117):

> Das Buch, in dem er gelesen hatte, stellte er genau immer wieder in
> den Schrein, aus dem er es genommen hatte, und wenn man gleich
> nach seinem Heraustritte in das Bücherzimmer ging, konnte man
> nicht im geringsten wahrnehmen, daß eben jemand hier gewesen sei,
> und gelesen habe. Überhaupt durfte bei dem Vater kein Zimmer die
> Spuren des unmittelbaren Gebrauches zeigen, sondern mußte immer
> aufgeräumt sein, als wäre es ein Prunkzimmer. (*NS* 8)

In Stifter's universe, whether passion is tacitly extolled or vocally cen-
sured, the fear of its power constantly underlies what Fischer defines as
the author's fundamental need for purity.[10]

However, human sexuality is not the only passionate urge that the
characters attempt to ward off by means of ritual behaviour. As Kaiser
recognises in his interpretation of "Der Kuß von Sentze," a subtext of
human *aggression* can equally be detected beneath the obsessively

orderly conduct of the family. Again, Kaiser relies too heavily on the account of neurosis offered by Freud (in this instance, he uses *Totem und Tabu* to try to explain the story), but he is surely quite right when he declares: "der Kuß von Sentze ist ein Familienritual zur Niederhaltung intrafamiliärer Aggressionen."[11] It is made evident at the start of the story that the "kiss of peace" functions as a rite that keeps "Haß und Feindschaft" in check (*GW* III: 699). As the narrator explains, it guarantees the maintenance of peace and order: "Die Streitenden konnten den Kuß verweigern, dazu hatten sie das Recht; haben sie ihn aber einmal gegeben, dann mußten sie Frieden halten" (*GW* III: 684). This formula thus curbs and contains aggression, but by no means eradicates it; indeed it may easily re-assert itself in sublimated form in the service of "self-restraint," the forcible suppression of one's own most powerful urges and emotions. This is the aggression both driving and lurking beneath the obsessive rituals in *Der Nachsommer*. Although it is controlled, violence is nonetheless inherent in the *Rosenhaus*. Heinrich, for example, is arrested by the "wahre Gewalt von Rosen" (*NS* 125), and Risach is not satisfied with merely casting aside the engravings that are of no use to him, but demands that they be destroyed ("Die schlechten Blätter wollte man dann vernichten," *NS* 603).

On a still deeper and darker level, however, the texts often imply something even more disturbing than suppressed sexuality or violence. "Abdias" (Abdias, 1847) is one such story, and the protagonist's obsessive security measures are particularly eloquent. On the most straightforward level, they afford protection against an external threat. Abdias takes elaborate precautions to ensure the security of his money and documents, but these precautions do not seem excessive when we have just witnessed his desert home being plundered by his enemy Melek. Likewise, it seems practical to install a lightning conductor to protect himself and Ditha against the elements. However, once he has moved to Europe, there *is* no external threat. As the narrator laconically reports: "es traf keine der gefürchteten Gefahren ein" (1,5: 296). Abdias makes his house in rural Austria even more secure than the one in Africa: it has double bolts on all the doors, heavy iron bars at all the windows, a massive wall to prevent intruders from getting into the garden, and it is completely protected against attacks from potential assailants ("von Außen gegen Angriffe geschützt," 1,5: 304–5). Melek, however, has been left far behind in Africa, and in this respect the narrator is right to see these measures as "lauter Anstalten, die er in Europa nicht nöthig hatte" (1,5: 304). At the same time, however, these measures are entirely necessary as the enemy is altogether real to Abdias's "inner eye," and disaster does indeed descend upon him, albeit by a

route different from the one he so elaborately guards against. But what exactly *is* this "enemy?" The text suggests that it is essentially *within*: the bars, walls and fences act as bastions against an unnamed and unnameable fear of his own wild nature, his "Wüstennatur" (1,2: 152). In the essay "Gartenlaube" (The Arbour, 1866) Stifter reflects upon the human desire to climb a tower or a hill in order to obtain a comprehensive overview (*MSB* 544), and he couples this with the equally strong desire to retreat to the apparent security of confined spaces (in terms that sound like a pre-echo of Nietzsche's "Der Mensch mit sich allein"):

> er [geht] auch wieder sehr gerne in kleine und beengte Gelasse, um mit sich selber allein zu sein, er geht in ein Gebüsch des Waldes oder Gartens, er geht in ein kleines schmales Tal, er geht in sein Kämmerlein, oder in seinen Erker, oder in sein Sommerhäuslein . . . Und je begrenzter und in sich geschlossener so ein Räumchen ist, um desto lieber sucht man es auf, damit der Mensch, um seiner andern Welt, der innern, wie klein sie auch sein möge, ein Zeitchen zu leben, von den äußeren Dingen desto sicherer abgetrennt sei. (*MSB* 544)

This is essentially what Abdias does; but once he is alone in his "inner world," his fear increases because he is forced to confront the horror of his inner abyss. He is in a crucial sense in the same plight as the creature in Kafka's story "Der Bau" (The Burrow, 1923–24; and this sense is reinforced by the narrator's coincidental reference to Abdias's house as "der . . . Bau," 1,5: 305). Like Kafka's creature, Abdias fills his days with manic, void-filling activity, taking endless if ultimately futile precautions against the tricks and treacheries of existence: "die Welt ist mannigfaltig und an schlimmen Überraschungen fehlt es niemals"[12]; it is in fact Kafka's animal that speaks these words, but they could just as easily have been written by Stifter.

On this level, *all* the rituals in Stifter's texts are essentially attempts to mask the void. In "Der Hagestolz," it is the locking ritual that governs the haggard uncle's life. He, too, is a dedicated collector, albeit in a grotesque variation on the theme: he has an entire repertoire of physical devices for protecting himself against an outer enemy. The word "Gitter" is crucial in this context: it occurs no fewer than fourteen times in thirteen pages (1,6: 68–81). He obsessively locks up his wine and cheese (1,6: 78); he imprisons Victor in his bedroom (1,6: 81); he locks his dogs away and suggests that Victor do the same (1,6: 80, 81); he even does his own shaving so that no one has the chance to slit his throat (1,6: 109). And yet there is no enemy. The only other inhabitants of the island are a couple of ancient servants and some mouldering stuffed birds. The narrator's comment about the manic locking in "Die

Narrenburg" could easily apply to the uncle: "es war lächerlich, zu
schließen, wo nichts zu verschließen war" (1,6: 374). In this respect,
the locking rituals indicate that, far from being at risk from any outside
forces, the man is an abject prisoner of his own neuroses. Winterstein
alleges that his fear of an accident with the razor "symbolisiert die Kas-
tration,"[13] whilst his fear of dogs supposedly expresses sexual desire for
his father ("Gefressenwerden . . . ist nur eine regressive Umsetzung des
Wunsches, vom Vater so befriedigt zu werden wie die Mutter").[14]
Needless to say, this is not what the text suggests. Even in the initial
chapter it is made clear that what the uncle fears is an untimely and
violent death. The old man is imprisoned by his dread of a "gewalt-
thätige Verkürzung seines Lebens" (1,6: 19), and it later becomes clear
that he embodies an extreme *existential* fear — a fear of an ultimate absence of meaning in either life or death: "Alles zerfällt im Augenblike,
wenn man nicht ein Dasein erschaffen hat, das über dem Sarge noch
fort dauert . . . Mit meinem Tode fällt alles dahin, was ich als ich gewesen bin — — — —" (1,6: 122-3). This excessive preoccupation partly
explains his advice to Victor that he should marry; advice that is almost
as obsessive as the locking rituals directed against an enemy who does
not exist.

A similar relationship between the characters' manic behaviour and
their terror of physical decline informs "Der Waldsteig." In the journal
version, it is made clear that Tiburius's fear of illness is far from normal
when the narrator refers to him as "der gründlichste hypochondrische
Narr und Grillenreiter" (1,3: 138). He is not explicitly accused of being
a hypochondriac in the book version. Instead, Stifter adopts a proce-
dure both more subtle and more telling: he greatly increases the
amount of detail devoted to Tiburius's collections. The same melan-
choly pervades the story, but it expresses itself as a subtext through his
objects; he uses them and their supposed inherent meaning in a desperate attempt to ward off his dread of a senseless death. Stifter's own obsessive tendencies display similar characteristics to those of Tiburius.
Whilst it is fruitless to indulge in crude psychoanalytical speculation
about an author, it nonetheless seems fair to remember the excess of
morbid anxiety about his health which Stifter recorded in "Mein Befinden." This fear is so overwhelming that it raises the suspicion that, like
the characters he creates, he is terrified by the thought of his death because the transcendence which he seeks to affirm is on one level only a
dream. It is striking, as Fischer has noted, that Stifter's obsession with
cacti and his manic fears about his health developed simultaneously
("Auffallend ist das Hinzutreten der 'Cactusnarrheit' . . . gleichzeitig
mit dem Auftreten der merkwürdigen psychosomatischen Zustände

1854/55")[15] — a pattern that re-enacts in real life what Stifter had already depicted in the book version of "Der Waldsteig," where Tiburius's hypochondriac father begins "eine Sammlung aller möglichen Cactusarten" (1,6: 147). It can scarcely be a coincidence that he shares this activity with his creator. Yet in both cases their fear remains unabated despite all their attempts to find solace and existential rootedness in these orderly collections.

Needless to say, the relentless predominance of fear in the lives of Stifter and his characters has decisive implications regarding the true status and significance of "things" within Stifter's world. I have already noted that Stifter uses physical objects to substantiate a purported faith that the universe is divinely underwritten. But the fact that the characters' fears cannot be assuaged by all their devotion to physical objects suggests that those objects may not after all be tokens and guarantors of divine order. On the contrary, they can exhibit a disturbingly random diversity, as exemplified in the repeated use of the epithet "verschieden" to depict the *Rentherr* and his belongings in "Turmalin" (2,2: 135–41) — an epithet that recurs in the evocations of Georg's butterfly collection in "Der Waldgänger," and the uncle's collection in "Der Hagestolz" (*GW* III: 403; 1,6: 76–8). These characters are three of the many who systematically amass objects in an attempt to confer wholeness on life and meaning on death. However, these "things" do not possess objective, inherent meaning: they are contingent ciphers of nothingness, pointing in this perspective to an absolute absence of signification in the world at large. Risach suggests as much when he declares — in terms reminiscent of those Stifter uses in "Der Tandelmarkt": "Die Voreltern legten so sehr einen eigentümlichen Geist in ihre Dinge — es war der Geist ihres Gemütes und ihres allgemeinen Gefühlslebens — daß sie diesem Geiste sogar den Zweck opferten" (*NS* 258). Even in *Der Nachsommer*, then, Stifter speaks of these "things" not in terms of their intrinsic meaning, but as being invested fetish-like with the spirit of their erstwhile possessors; as such they become a kind of venerable repository of life after death. In this respect, the *Hagestolz*'s fear of death throws a disturbing light on the making of objects into fetishes in stories such as "Die Mappe": the childless Stifter resorts to "things" as the enduring palladium of individuals' spirit and essence.[16]

This is reflected particularly clearly in "Der Waldgänger," one of Stifter's bleakest stories. The solitary Georg is a dedicated collector throughout the story, but his collecting is of a different order from the collecting undertaken by characters such as Risach or the "Kalkstein" priest: Georg's collecting is directly related to a fear of the abyss rather than suppressed sexuality. Georg's sense of overwhelming existential

emptiness is most graphically revealed by his collection of stones. A clear symbolic link is established by the fact that he accumulates and categorises more and more stones as it becomes increasingly obvious that he and Corona can never have children. This connection is emphasised after the barren couple spend an evening with acquaintances and their children, particularly by the deviously telling use of the verb "sammeln": the others at the party "collect" their children around them while Georg and Corona are left alone ("Als . . . die betreffenden Mütter ihre Kinder um sich sammelten, . . . so saßen Georg und Corona . . . allein," *GW* III: 476–7). The use of the verb "ordnen" is equally cunning. The other women put their children's clothes to rights ("Die . . . Mütter . . . gaben Auskunft, gaben Rede, und ordneten nebstbei etwas an dem verschobenen Gewändchen") while Corona looks on from her vantage-point of absolute isolation ("Corona saß vereinsamt und vereinzelt da, und schaute zu," *GW* III: 474). She, too, eradicates supposed disarray, but the object of her manic attentions is her *house*, not human beings. She scours and orders everything that is already clean and orderly; she scrubs away almost non-existent dust ("Dann beseitigte sie den wenigen Staub, der seit gestern gekommen," *GW* III: 462); she obsessively orders and re-orders her possessions (the word "Ordnung" appears in one form or another no fewer than eight times in two pages, *GW* III: 470–2). Georg, moreover, returns home to his collection of stones, his ersatz children ("heute hatte er sich — man weiß keinen Grund — von der Arbeit weg begeben und war zu seinen Steinen gegangen") and communes with them as if they were human ("Zudem siehst du ja, daß ich . . . gleichsam mit diesem Steine da rede," *GW* III: 477–8). The build-up to the couple's separation begins at precisely this point, and it reaches its conclusion several pages later in a particularly subtle yet graphic use of stone symbolism: their union sundered in all but name, Georg and Corona encounter the men busily rendering their garden both larger and more fecund by cleansing the new tranche of its sterile detritus of stones ("gereinigt, von Steinen befreit," *GW* III: 484). This hint of liberation and heightened fertility appears to be borne out when Georg goes on to father children with a different woman; but his manic collecting continues unabated, for in truth nothing can fill his inner void. That Corona's plight is essentially the same is shown with chilling force even in the depiction of her early upbringing: possessions are heaped upon her; her rooms are bursting with mirrors, jewels, caskets, and fabrics — and all this in order that she encounter "keine . . . Leere" (*GW* III: 448). But what the plethora of possessions actually expresses is the magnitude of her *inner* emptiness.

Both obsessive orderliness and the accumulation of objects take us
beyond sexuality and clearly imply a vision in which man's existence has
no inherent meaning. Although Stifter's will to portray unambiguously
meaningful "things" is clearly as great as his will to create unambiguously meaningful symbols, the texts record the breakdown of both. The
disorderly abundance of physical objects in "Der Waldgänger" comes to
signify the abyssal chaos inherent in those who collect them. Fischer
recognises that objects are portrayed as much for their relationship to
subjective man as for their "objektive Giltigkeit" and he remarks of
Stifter: "Es geht ihm nicht mehr um die Dinge, wie sie sind, um ihre
Klarheit, sondern um Erhaltung der Klarheit in sich selbst, die er um den
Preis der Ding-Überhöhung zuwege bringt."[17] The all-encompassing
"wholeness" which Stifter, through Heinrich, postulates in *Der Nachsommer* (*NS* 285) is in this perspective as much a shimmering mirage as
the "salvation" that Abdias hopes to find (1,5: 259). The characters attempt by means of objects to put a splintered existence back together
again, but the meaninglessness inherent in the objects that they use
only reinforces the terrifyingly shattered nature both of their own being
and of Being *per se*. This is what Stern recognises when he aptly remarks
of Stifter's "things": "And so they become, not symbols of human
values and dignity, but fetishes of Stifter's own fears."[18]

With this in mind, it is interesting to return to two stories that deal
with this personal-cum-existential fear in strikingly similar terms, namely
"Der Hagestolz" and "Der Waldsteig" (written within weeks of one
another). Like Tiburius in "Der Waldsteig," the reclusive uncle is characterised by mistrust, and the detritus with which both characters surround themselves defies rational comprehension. A further analogy can
be drawn between the two collections in that they are both partly
driven by sexual passion (the uncle shuts himself off and amasses objects
after being sexually betrayed, and, as suggested earlier, Tiburius's sexual
energy is displaced into his drive to collect). However, Tiburius's psy-
chological disturbance is ultimately resolved when he learns to love
Maria, and his hypochondria duly melts away. "Der Hagestolz" offers a
far less conciliatory vision,[19] and it is a superior story because the objects
that make up the uncle's dwelling are not merely tokens of the breakdown of reason or morality but provide a haunting subtextual expression of an existence without essence; they suggest dimensions of mania
matched by very few stories.

If we now look at the actual objects gathered by the characters, we
see that Tiburius's collections are to a certain extent a remake of those
of the uncle. The narrators in both stories, for example, focus on the
characters' pipe collections (1,6: 152 and 1,6: 87 respectively). How-

ever, where Tiburius's collection is disturbing because it reveals his inability to reason and categorise, the uncle's is unsettling because it serves only to blank out the void. In the essay "Über unsere gegenwärtige Lage und unsere sittliche Verbesserung" (On Our Present Situation and Our Moral Improvement, 1849), Stifter declares: "Es ist ein natürliches Ding, daß der Mensch, der einfach und mäßig lebt, der nicht immer auf Erheiterung seines Körpers denkt, Zeit und Muße hat, seine Seele auf das Höhere zu richten" (*GW* VI: 339). To my mind, no story goes against the grain of this faith so radically as "Der Hagestolz." The uncle's collection is sheer decaying matter with no inherent meaning, pointing indirectly to the senselessness of the man's crumbling existence and his looming extinction: he has been swallowed up by his own mania, he has descended into the abyss, "das Unbedeutende Leere und Nichtige" (*NS* 374). More perturbingly than perhaps any other story, the whole obsessive lifestyle played out on the uncle's ultramundane island expresses utter negativity, the terrifying disintegration of all that is and can be known to man.[20] The narrator insists on this when Victor first surveys the awesome vista of the lake and its surroundings: he can see "Nicht ein Häuschen, nicht einen Menschen, nicht ein einziges Thier"; he can discern "nicht einen einzigen Lichtfunken"; there is "gar nichts zu verspüren"; and he is, eloquently, surrounded by "lichte Dinge, die er nicht kannte" (1,6: 61). The extreme sense of negativity envisaged on the island itself is, moreover, indicated by the suggestion that God, the ultimate guarantor of the "essence of things," is absent: the monastery is in ruins; the peal of the mainland church bells does not reach the silent island; Victor forgets to say his prayers. What Stifter offers here is a realm of "Unmaß," a realm of complete emptiness and otherness that even the most frantic collecting and cleansing could never adequately mask. We are transported with Victor into a zone that is entirely symbolic, a God-forsaken, chasmic dimension beyond the known that calls to mind other fictive landscapes such as the mountain in "Bergkristall," and the Puszta in "Brigitta." The otherness of this dystopia is reinforced by one of Stifter's most telling depictions of a complete loss of orientation. Victor finds himself in an alien world where he loses all sense of time and space; he wonders where Ludmilla's house is but cannot decide: "Er hatte nehmlich . . . die Richtung der Weltgegenden verloren" (1,6: 82). And this vision is not confined to the external world: it is an eloquently silent intimation of bleak possibilities in man himself that defy direct expression. The repeated use of words such as "unsäglich" and "unermeßlich" makes it clear that we have reached the marginal zones of what is sayable or knowable (1,6: 103, 113, 54). We are led into the unspeakable abyss of

which man's existence consists. *This* is the realm that Stifter obsessively portrays beneath the surface so moderate and tranquil; *this* is the realm where his true fascination lies.

Notes

[1] Schumacher, "Nachwort," in Stifter, *Briefe*, 533.

[2] Schumacher, "Nachwort," 529.

[3] Matz, *Adalbert Stifter*, 138.

[4] Rudolf Wildbolz, *Adalbert Stifter: Langeweile und Faszination* (Stuttgart: Kohlhammer, 1976), 10.

[5] Wildbolz, *Langeweile und Faszination*, 10.

[6] Wildbolz, *Langeweile und Faszination*, 10.

[7] The last thing that Victor sees of "home" is, moreover, the *red* of Ludmilla's roof ("so roth . . . wie Hannas Tuch," 1,6: 53).

[8] Reddick, "Tiger und Tugend," 241, 245, 249, 250, 251.

[9] See the short story "Zuversicht" (Confidence, 1846, *GW* III: 808).

[10] Fischer, "Psychologische Beiträge," 102.

[11] Kaiser, *Adalbert Stifter*, 107.

[12] Franz Kafka, *Die Erzählungen* ([Frankfurt am Main], 1961), 401.

[13] Winterstein, *Adalbert Stifter: Persönlichkeit und Werk*, 160.

[14] Winterstein, *Adalbert Stifter: Persönlichkeit und Werk*, 160.

[15] Fischer, "Psychologische Beiträge," 85.

[16] The importance that Stifter attached to children in existential terms is suggested by a letter to Heckenast written in early 1846, in which he claims that only those people who have children live on after their deaths: "es ist ein Naturgesetz, daß Menschen sterben, und haben sie recht gelebt, und ihr Alter in Kindern verherrlicht, so sterben sie nicht ganz" (*MSB* 668). Again, this casts his object-fetishism in an unsettling light.

[17] Fischer, "Psychologische Beiträge," 71.

[18] Stern, *Reinterpretations*, 297.

[19] Blackall again misses the point: "Stifter never wrote a more insistent affirmation of life than *Der Hagestolz*" (*Adalbert Stifter*, 201).

[20] For a short but detailed and convincing consideration of "Der Hagestolz," see John Reddick, "The Wild Beyond: Symbolic Journeyings in the Stories of Adalbert Stifter," *Oxford German Studies*, 20/21 (1991–92): 112–16.

3: Ritual in Style

> "Sie mag es wohl fühlen, daß hinter dem pedantischen Krame,
> wie sie ihn nennt, wohl mehr stecke, als sie ahnte"
>
> ("Die Mappe meines Urgroßvaters")

[Kafkas Dichtungen] sind erfüllt von einer vernünftigen, wenn auch ironisch-, ja satirisch-vernünftigen, verzweifelt vernünftigen, nach bester Kraft auf das Gute, Rechte und Gottgewollte gerichteten Sittlichkeit, welche sich schon in ihrem gewissenhaft-sachlichen, sonderbar ausführlichen, korrekten und klaren, durch einen genauen und beinahe amtlichen Konservatismus oft geradezu an Adalbert Stifter erinnernden Vortragsstil malt.[1]

THOMAS MANN'S COMPARISON proves highly relevant at this point in the argument. In exploring Stifter's portrayal of his characters and their collections, we have seen how a crucial tension is everywhere apparent. On the surface of the texts, we find characters and objects that appear to uphold an ethos of moderation, unambiguous "normality," and order based on absolutes such as reason, morality and God. At the same time, we find that the self-same objects tell a different story: one of mania, of eccentric obsession, where the leading role is played by the unspeakable ambiguity of darkness, sensualism, and contingency. As Thomas Mann clearly recognises, however, this dual vision is not confined to Stifter's subject-matter. It finds equally powerful expression in the *manner* of his writing, and it is accordingly his style — distinctive and ultimately extreme — that I now want to explore.

Without doubt, one of the main themes of Stifter's stories is the way in which rational man attempts to perceive categorical order in the objects that make up the world around him. But such considerations are not simply part of the subject-matter: Stifter also endeavours to convey order and reason through his narrative style. On the surface of the texts, order is apparently the broad governing principle of the cosmos, and this seems to be not only thematically but also stylistically validated. It is particularly useful to look both at Stifter's representation of dialogue and at the descriptive methods deployed in his later prose.[2] Taken at face value, the way in which he uses dialogue suggests the incontrovertibility of order as much as does the subject-matter. "Der fromme

Spruch," for example, takes us into a world where order is to a large extent upheld by the ceremonial exchanges between the ageing Dietwin and Gerlint. A similar immutable order is enshrined in the many descriptive passages by the use of a language so rhythmically grave and simple that it acquires the supplicatory force of litany — a tendency in Stifter that, along with the amount of textual space devoted to dialogue, increases markedly in the later works. His evocation of the Drendorf household in *Der Nachsommer* offers us just one of the countless examples of this style:

> Die obere Stufe ist gewissermaßen das Prunkzimmer. In ihr stehen die schöneren Betten des Hauses, gewöhnlich zwei, in ihr stehen die Schreine mit den schönen Kleidern, in ihr hängen die Scheiben- und Jagdgewehre des Mannes . . . in ihr sind die schöneren Geschirre der Frau . . . und in ihr sind auch die besseren Bilder des Hauses. (*NS* 24)

Significantly, though, this technique is not confined solely to the latter part of the oeuvre, but is also a salient feature of the revisions that he makes to earlier works. In the journal version of "Turmalin," for example, the language used to convey the *Rentherr*'s repeated visits to Dall is relatively unfocussed, even rambling:

> als er bei allen Freunden und Bekannten gefragt hatte, und diese nichts wußten, ging er zu *Dall* . . . Da dieser die nämliche Antwort ertheilte, kam der Rentherr in mehreren Tagen einigemale, und wiederholte dasselbe . . . Endlich kam der Rentherr nicht mehr. (2,1: 117)

The book version recounts exactly the same actions, but with a driving simplicity, a kind of rhythmic minimalism of language that renders them almost frightening; "less" here is emphatically "more":

> Er ging zu Dall, und . . . ging nach Hause. Nach einiger Zeit kam er wieder zu Dall . . . Nach einigen Tagen kam er abermals . . . Der Rentherr kam nach einigen Tagen noch einmal . . . Dann kam er nicht mehr. (2,2: 144–5)

I suggest that this increasingly litaneutic mode is the stylistic equivalent of the collecting motif. Like the characters' collections of physical objects, it reflects on one level an attempt at control[3]: nothing could be more measured and controlled than this solemn prose. As I shall show, however, it simultaneously suggests quite the opposite.

I noted earlier that the events in Stifter's stories unfold with a gradualness that seems to illustrate his explicit faith in reflection and restraint, in a life within which everything proceeds "in gewissem Maße" (*MSB* 523). This thematic strategy of advancing by degrees is expressive of man's capacity rationally to achieve the mature "overview over a

greater whole" postulated in the *Bunte Steine* preface. We find the same, as it were sacral, progression of events duplicated in the style, the linguistic repetitions in both the dialogue and the narrative seeming to mirror "die gewöhnlichen alltäglichen in Unzahl wiederkehrenden Handlungen der Menschen" that apparently preserve "das Gesez des Rechtes und der Sitte" (2,2: 14). Such gradualness is in turn related to the accomplishment of the kind of unambiguous objectivity associated with the scientist or "Forscher" (2,2: 10). We already know that a number of the characters have a scientific or scholarly bent, implying that they have achieved the reverential objectivity that is praised in the preface. However, it is perhaps even more significant that the increasing repetition and stylisation in Stifter's mode of expression likewise seem to suggest such objectivity. This trend towards an air of objectivity is, for example, implied by the increasing avoidance of colloquial expression in the dialogue of works such as "Die Mappe." There are numerous colourful exchanges between the students Augustinus and Eustachius in the journal version of this story, such as "Ey, ey, Felsensteine und Herzklopfen ... sie sagen ohnedem auf dem Carolin, sie bohre dir den Gecken" and "Nun Kaukasus und Cedernbäume ... ehe ich dich aufreibe, zeige einmal, wie dieß zu nehmen ist" (1,2: 46–7); all are effaced during the process of revision. Furthermore, the almost pedantic tendency in the *Letzte Mappe* to use constructions such as "in dem Gange" and "von dem Amte" (rather than "im Gange" or "vom Amte") suggests a desire to guard against ambiguity.[4] It might seem as if Stifter is, so to speak, filling all the gaps, giving us a plausible and seamless interpretation of the world as a categorisable whole. His propensity to use lists in the later works could likewise be viewed as a stylistic reflection of the listable, knowable universe.[5] Thus we are given lists of people ("Der Vater der Kaspar die Anna der Knecht die Mägde der Stallbub," *MSB* 60); of places ("Ich ging ... nach Italien; nach Venedig Florenz Rom Neapel Syrakus Palermo Malta ... Ich war in Gibraltar Granada Sevilla Cordoba Toledo Madrid," *NS* 708); and of objects ("Er hatte Münzen, er hatte Siegel, er hatte keltische und römische Altertümer, Musikgeräte Tulpen und Georginen Bücher Gemälde und Bildsäulen," *NS* 460).[6] This mode — on one level at least — expresses that thrust of the ideology of reason that proposes that the world can be classified and organised into controllable, static categories; it is the linguistic expression of the ethos underlying the fictive objects that the characters collect.

As I have suggested, however, Stifter is not solely concerned with man's ability to exert intellectual control over the external world, but also with his ability to exert moral control over the forces within him.

Again, particularly if we compare the different versions of the stories, we find that the style articulates this concern. The revised versions are characterised by a stylistic tendency to tone down and objectivise the characters' passionate outbursts, and to simplify the language in the passages that deal with complex emotions. Revealing in this respect are the changes made to the scene present only in the two later versions of "Die Mappe" in which Augustinus ventures to declare his feelings for Margarita. In the book version, the style, with its plethora of dashes, bespeaks Augustinus's breathlessly passionate excitement:

> — — Da fragte ich Margarita, ob sie mich recht liebe. — — — — Margarita, als sie meine Frage vernommen hatte, schlug die Augenlieder über die sehr schönen braunen Augen herab, sah in die Schäftchen nieder, wurde ganz glüh im Angesichte, und schüttelte leise das Haupt. — — Ich sagte kein Wort, und wir gingen auf dem Wege wieder dahin. (1,5: 167–8)

The corresponding passage of the *Letzte Mappe* is, in contrast, marked by a strongly monodic style, suggesting that *this* Augustinus conceives his passion in far more restrained and moderate terms. The fevered dashes all disappear, and Augustinus delivers instead a passage with a slow but unmistakably rhythmic pulse, achieved above all by that ever more frequent device of Stifter's, linguistic iteration: the verb "gehen" echoes and re-echoes six times within this handful of lines:

> Wir gingen auf dem breiten Wege neben einander, und ich legte ihren Arm sanft in den meinigen. Da wir so gingen, fragte ich: "Margarita, habt Ihr mich doch auch ein wenig lieb?"
> Sie antwortete auf diese Frage nicht, und wir gingen langsam unseres Weges weiter. Sie schlug die Lider über ihre großen Augen nieder, sah in die feinen Halme, die an unserem Wege wuchsen, und allerlei graues und silbernes Flinselwerk trugen, wurde ganz glüh im Angesichte, und schüttelte dann unmerklich das Haupt. Den Arm aber, welchen ich in den meinigen gelegt hatte, ließ sie mir. Wir gingen zu dem Kalkofen hinunter. Dort sagten sie uns, der Herr Obrist sei schon lange in das Haus hinauf gegangen. Wir gingen also wieder zurück, und sprachen beinahe kein Wort. (*MSB* 150)

The more measured, more rhythmical phrases signify a drastic diminution in subjectivity, serving almost to remove the experience from its personal context in a way that clearly shows the affinity between the *Letzte Mappe*, *Der Nachsommer*, and *Witiko*.

The same movement towards measure and restraint seems to characterise the development of the dialogue throughout the oeuvre. Peter Branscombe is one of the few critics who have examined this aspect of Stifter's style in any depth and, in his article entitled "Some Reflections

on the Use of Dialogue in Stifter's Stories," he makes some telling points.[7] He comments on the differences between the two versions of "Brigitta," with particular reference to the exchange between Brigitta and Stephan that marks their separation. As Branscombe recognises, Stephan's outburst in the journal version: "ich hasse dich, ich hasse dich" (1,2: 245) becomes the literally unspeakable: "ich hasse dich unaussprechlich" in the book version (1,5: 459). In one sense, he is quite right to say that this manner of speaking is "less likely to be thought appropriate to speech in the given circumstances" than its predecessor.[8] However, he has perhaps missed the point when he claims that the change represents an "overt intensification of emotion."[9] On the contrary, it appears that Stifter means to present us with an overt and deliberate *de*intensification of emotion. The same dispassion seems to mark the words that Stifter places in Mathilde's mouth in *Der Nachsommer* upon her learning that she and Risach are to separate: "Schwer oder nicht schwer, von dem ist hier nicht die Rede . . . , von dem, was sein muß, ist die Rede, von dem, dessen Gegenteil ich für unmöglich hielt" (*NS* 667). The passionate despair that we might anticipate is moderated by the formal syntax and the tolling of the words "von dem," these elements again apparently showing the style to be the organ of moral restraint. Whether the aim of restraint is achieved in practice remains to be seen, but there seems little doubt that such stylistic developments express a determination on Stifter's part to suppress subjective emotion, or at any rate to remove all sign of it from the surface of his narratives.

This style, however, articulates by no means solely an ethos of moral self-control, laudable though this may be. What the combined features of Stifter's aesthetic demonstrate is perhaps a kind of classicising process.[10] The dialogue in *Der Nachsommer* between Heinrich and Risach, for example, generally comes across — most aptly in the context of this seemingly Apollonian novel — as statuesque and sacral, as we see in this exchange between the two characters, an exchange that, pertinently, refers to the statue:

"Ich habe nämlich den Glauben, daß das Bildwerk sehr schön sei," antwortete ich mich verbessernd.

"Ich teile mit Euch den Glauben, daß das Werk von großer Bedeutung sei," sagte er.

"Und warum habt Ihr denn nie zu mir darüber gesprochen?" fragte ich.

"Weil ich dachte, daß Ihr es nach einer bestimmten Zeit selber betrachten und für schön erachten werdet," antwortete er.

"Wenn Ihr mir es früher gesagt hättet, so hätte ich es früher gewußt," erwiderte ich. (*NS* 328)[11]

As we have seen, the statue is incorporated into the textual canvas partly to capture the ethical connotations of the pure white marble and partly as a visual realisation of the "essence of things." It is this same combination that Stifter endeavours to achieve through his use of language. I have already noted that he attempts to express moral temperance in his restrained style, but equally significant is the way in which this mode endeavours to enact the essence within objects. One of the primary stylistic ways in which he contends that things unquestioningly and rightly "are" is by using the verb "sein" in a non-predicative manner. His increasing tendency to employ this device is particularly clearly demonstrated by the changes made in "Granit." The passage in the journal version in which the grandfather points out the inhabitants of the forest to his young grandson reads:

> Die Einen sind Holzknechte . . . die andern sind Kohlenbrenner . . . die andern sind Heuarbeiter . . . die letzten sind endlich die Pechbrenner. (2,1: 20)

In the corresponding passage in "Granit," the litaneutical way in which he uses "sein" shows him striving to intimate the language of pure being:

> Da sind zuerst die Holzknechte . . . Dann sind die Kohlenbrenner . . . Dann sind die Heusucher . . . Dann sind die Sammler . . . Endlich sind die Pechbrenner. (2,2: 34–5)

This is what Stern refers to as Stifter's "ontic" mode,[12] and it is what Herbert Seidler has in mind when he claims: "so enthüllt und entfaltet sich im *sein* das Sein überhaupt, das Dasein in dieser Schöpfung."[13] It appears to be the stylistic equivalent of the transcendence that seems embodied in Risach's collection of marble, suggesting the unshakeable security of existence in the God-given universe and the ultimate possibility of unambiguous meaning.

By using such a measured and objectivised style, Stifter seeks aesthetically to maintain the ethos of reason according to which man can organise the universe into static, controllable categories. As I commented earlier, though, there is a major strand of his creativity which suggests that human reason can never fully penetrate the world without, and that perverse objects defy all attempts to grasp their meaning. In this context, I noted an inclination towards excess in the characters' collections that ultimately serves to problematise notions of the power and sovereignty of human reason. This tendency towards extremes or even excess is, moreover, something that Stifter recognised (at least to some degree) in himself. In a letter of 4 July 1830 to Mathias Greipl, he expresses his acute awareness

daß ich die Grenzen eines heiter ruhigen Lebens überschreiten, und in Extreme fallen könnte, welche die Harmonie in Wildheit, und Sitte in Unordnung herabstürzen, und indem sie die Wunde nur betäuben, dieselbe nicht nur nicht heilen, sondern vergrößern, und aus einem Unglücklichen einen Sünder machen. (*MSB* 631)

If we turn again to the style with this in mind, we find that similar hidden depths can be readily discerned. Martin and Erika Swales recognise some of these submerged tendencies when they write of the rigid style of "Der fromme Spruch": "this petrification is the extreme product of Stifter's ideology of reason, his unceasing and ever-increasing determination to build texts which would stand as unshakeable houses of meaning."[14] They put their finger here on one of the crucial features of Stifter's later work: its stylistic extremism. As with the objects amassed by his characters, the moderation in his style very frequently tips over into mania; the stylistic message that reason must and does prevail is too vehement to be convincing. This is surely what Thomas Mann had in mind when, mentioning the Stifter-like tenor of Kafka's style, he particularly highlighted the element of "*verzweifelt* vernünftige Sittlichkeit." Klatt detects a similar pattern. He acknowledges "die große Ruhe und das klare Ebenmaß von Stifters Stil," but sees it as wholly contrived ("gewollt, ja fast erzwungen"), the product of profound inner turbulence and despair.[15] We may be lulled by Stifter's style into believing that he upholds human reason, but part of the inescapable tension of his works lies in his almost obsessive attempt to preserve reason in the teeth of the fear that man's cognitive capabilities are actually hopelessly limited.

One could go so far as to suggest that Stifter deploys style as a desperate means to control the external events and objects that humans cannot control despite their vaunted possession of reason. This leads to a pervasive tension between a sense of incomprehensible chaos in the world at large, and a sense of extreme order implacably conveyed through the language. This is another stylistic tendency that Stifter shares with Kafka. In this respect, it is significant that both writers eked out a tedious living by working for the sprawling Austro-Hungarian bureaucracy. They both had to produce official reports using the notoriously rigid *Amtssprache* (Kafka on industrial safety matters, and Stifter in his capacity as an Inspector of Schools). Kafka, furthermore, was obliged to compile rational lists of the most horrific catastrophes in his handling of the disability and death claims of workers and their families, an antinomy that reveals itself in his literary mode.[16] Stifter may not have shared the latter task, but there is nonetheless a similarly desperate calmness in the style he uses to report mass disaster. In *Witiko*, for

example, the dialogue between the protagonist and Andreas lists in the most obsessively measured and matter-of-fact terms the names of the dead and the causes of their deaths:

> [Andreas] las: "Melchior von der Stift. Er ward durch und durch gestochen. Wenzel aus den Auhäusern. Er hatte die Wunde im Halse. Kaspar von Reichenau. Ich weiß nicht mehr, David, war es der mit dem zerbrochenen Kopfe?" . . .
>
> Andreas las weiter: "Michael von dem schwarzen Bache. Johannes aus den Heurafelwaldhäusern. Arnold von der unteren Moldau. Jobst von dem Rathschlage. Sebastian aus Friedberg. Ruprecht vom Kirchenschlage. Simon von Mugrau." (5,3: 54–5)

There is a disturbing gap between the style, which hammers home the notion that man can confer reason upon events, and the subject-matter, which points to a meaning beyond man's comprehension (a gap that moreover gives rise to a kind of deathly, absurdist humour). A similar feature marks the *Rentherr*'s repeated visits to Dall that, despite the incessant driving simplicity of the language, suggesting reason and control, result in ever starker incomprehension. In this technique, there is something akin not only to Kafka but also to Kleist: a mode of supreme control that serves to portray the actual or potential uncontrollability of matter.

The superlative control that characterises Stifter's style, however, does not relate solely to the ability or otherwise of humans to apply their reason. In Chapter One I suggested that there is, for Stifter, an undeniable connection between the outer world of objects and the characters' inner compulsions, and I argued that the excess of rational control in both cases came to signify a profound fear of *loss* of control. Perhaps even more significant, however, is that Stifter expresses precisely the same fears through his use of language. As I have suggested, the style is highly regulated in the passages that concern human passions, this on the surface pointing to an aesthetic of moral self-restraint ("Maß, Beherrschung, sittliche Organisierung," *MSB* 681). However, whilst the language is apparently toned down and objectivised, its very moderation, like man's "self-mastery," comes across as excessive; the human heart at the core of the stories beats all the more passionately because of the extreme composure of a style that attempts to exclude it. This feature is evident in "Der Waldgänger," for example, a story marked by subterranean feelings of consuming passion and corrosive loneliness. Nowhere else in the story are these feelings more powerfully or more poignantly expressed than in the exchange between Corona and Georg that takes place years after their separation. This colloquy is marked by its reasonable, tranquil style which implies their self-control:

"Corona," sagte er.

"Georg," antwortete sie. . . .

"Geht es dir wohl, Georg?"

"Wohl, Corona — dir auch?"

"Ja, Georg. — — Das ist eine schöne Gegend, nicht wahr?"

"Ja, sie ist schön — — sehr schön — — bist du lange hier, oder reisest du bloß durch?"

"Ich lebe schon mehrere Jahre in dem kleinen Städchen dort — du reisest wohl eben hier durch?"

"Ich bin in dem einzelnen Gasthause über Nacht."

"Reisest du dann wieder weiter?"

"Ja."

"Georg — — sage — ich möchte fragen: sind diese deine Kinder?"

"Ja, Corona."

"Wie alt sind sie denn?"

"Der eine ist neun, der andere zehn Jahre alt."

"Es sind freundliche Kinder. — Weil du nur Kinder erhalten hast."

"Bist du auch vermählt, Corona?"

"Es haben sich Anträge gefunden."

"Also bist du vermählt?"

Sie wurde sehr rot und sagte: "Ich habe es nicht vermocht."

Er antwortete kein Wort — nicht ein einziges Wort sagte er auf diese Rede. (GW III: 490)

This measured verbal intercourse, with its elementary, restrained language ("haben," "fragen," "sagen," and "sein" are the principal verbs), along with the lack of "stage directions" explicitly describing the characters' emotions, may seem to moderate the force of their passion. However, this mode of seemingly unruffled objectivity, with its quietly repetitive registration of the beauty of the scenery, again appears excessive. In effect, it serves to betray the intense passion and irremediable isolation of both characters by so insistently drawing attention to what is not being said. This, I believe, is where part of the supreme effectiveness of the alterations made to "Brigitta" lies. As I have indicated, the changes in the discourse between Brigitta and Stephan perform the overt function of petrifying their heated emotions. Yet their passion becomes more potently vulcanic in the book version because the restrained mode forces it underground. Here, we are again offered a passion that is conspicuous through the virtual *absence* of explicit passion in the style that conveys it. However, even more crucial — and even more unsettling — is that the Major's utterance "Weib, ich hasse

dich unaussprechlich" is an endeavour to express a passion that cannot *be* expressed in its full intensity.

Of equal significance, though, is that Stephan is made to declare his feelings not once but twice: "Weib, ich hasse dich unaussprechlich, ich hasse dich unaussprechlich!" (1,5: 459). This fact takes me to one of the most important aspects of Stifter's style, whereby the more over-whelming the underlying passion, the greater is his tendency towards stylistic iteration. This, of course, is strikingly similar to the behavioural rituals undertaken by those characters who try to "leash their inner tigers." As we know, one of the most significant aspects of their fictive behaviour is that the more compulsively ritualistic it becomes, the more excessive is the passion that underlies it. More crucially, however, the same story of excessive passion and obsessive ritual is told by the mode of expression: the more litaneutically bound it seems, the more bound-less is the passion it attempts to control — and the more menacing it becomes to the reader. This process becomes particularly evident if one compares the scene in all three versions of "Die Mappe" in which Augustinus contemplates suicide. In the journal version Stifter makes little attempt to hide the character's despair and rage; he even has him refer directly to his suicidal intentions:

> An einem sehr schönen Maytage nemlich — es war der vier und zwanzigste — stand ich sinnend vor einer alten Birke mit zartjungen Blättern und Zweigen, des festen Willens, mich daran zu erhängen. — Ein Weib, ein schönes, schnödes, fürchterlich geliebtes Weib hatte mich dermaßen rasend gemacht, daß ich vermeinte, jetzt könne ich nicht mehr weiter leben, um es nur recht zu strafen das falsche, das harte Herz. Als ich alle Kraft der Rede verschwendet und gesagt hatte, was nur zwischen Himmel und Erde zu sagen möglich war, und sie unerschüttert blieb, lief ich ungesäumt in den Wald zu einer wohl-bekannten Birkenstelle. (1,2: 15)

The book version demonstrates some attempt to subdue the passion, but Augustinus's torment is nonethless clearly conveyed by verbs such as "laufen," "zerreißen," "springen," and "dringen"; his intention to hang himself is also still explicit:

> ich [lief] in den Wald, an welcher Stelle eine Birke steht, und wollte mich daran erhängen . . . sie sollte es nur sehen, daß ich alles zerreiße und daß ich sie strafe, das falsche, wankelmüthige Herz . . . Ich lief von ihr in mein Haus, riß ein buntes Tuch von dem Tische, lief durch den Garten, sprang über den Zaun, und schnitt dann den Weg ab . . . Ich hatte aus dem Tuche eine Schlinge gemacht, und trug es in dem Busen versteckt. Dann beugte ich wieder links von dem Wege ab, strebte unter den dünnen Stämmen des ausgebrannten Waldes der

Dürrschnäbel hinauf, drang durch den Saum des Kirmwaldes, streifte an dem Stangenholze, an den Tannenbüschen, an den Felsblöcken vorbei und sprang auf den Platz hinaus, wo die vielen Birken stehen und der grüne Rasen dahingeht. (1,5: 33–4)

The *Letzte Mappe* is markedly different. There is no explicit mention of suicide, nor indeed are feelings of any kind explicitly named. Instead, we find an obsessive repetition of "ging" (eight times in one short passage), and a subtle yet arresting process whereby Augustinus's inner state is no longer directly evoked, but prismatically reflected in the horror he registers in the *external* world (the "fürchterliche Dinge" glinting in the sunshine, the fearful song of the blackbird):

Ich ging in unser Haus, blieb aber auch da nicht, sondern ging durch unsern Garten hinaus, dann hinter ihm durch das Obstgehege, stieg über die versperrte Tür der Verplankung, und ging durch das Gras der Wiese gegen den Pfad, der durch die Mitterwegfelder zu dem Birkenreut hinauf führt. Auf dem Pfade ging ich an den Kornfeldern des Friedmeier und Katermeier empor, und ging dann durch die Öffnung der Steinmauer in das Reut hinaus, wo auf dem Rasen die Wacholderbüsche stehen, und weiter zurück lauter Birken, und wo die Steinwand so hin und hin zieht. Ich ging unter die Birken, und setzte mich auf einen Stock. Auf der Steinwand glänzten fürchterliche Dinge und Flimmer in der Sonne, und eine Ammer sang mit der dünnen Stimme schreckhaft neben mir. Ich stand auf, und ging zu einer andern Stelle, und setzte mich auf einen Stein. Da war es mir, als hörte ich ein Geräusch. Ich sah um, und der Obrist ging auf mich zu. (*MSB* 159–60)

Far from implying moderation and restraint, this oblique, elliptical mode is infinitely more evocative and suggestive than the direct, "full-frontal" mode. It is, moreover, particularly significant that Augustinus's intended suicide is the result of a *sexual* trauma, as it is sexuality in particular that tends to be conveyed by means of this kind of language. We see that the style becomes accordingly more ritualistic in the exchanges between the male and female characters. Stifter's later tendency to use such linguistic rituals is already foreshadowed in the book version of "Brigitta," where Stephan's double declaration of hatred is preceded by the equally passionate Brigitta's ominously repetitive declaration: "Ich habe es dir gesagt, daß es dich reuen wird, ich habe es dir gesagt, daß es dich reuen wird" (1,5: 459).[17] A similar linguistic duplication characterises Heinrich's and Natalie's avowal of mutal love in *Der Nachsommer*:

"Ewig für dich allein," sagte ich.
"Ewig für dich allein," sagte sie leise. (*NS* 491)

Significantly, the repetition is not limited to these two lines. The dialogue in this scene is also a linguistic echo of the arresting oath of passion sworn by the young Risach and Mathilde:

> "Mathilde, dein auf immer und auf ewig, nur dein allein, und nur dein nur dein allein!"
>
> "O ewig dein, ewig, ewig, Gustav, dein, nur dein, und nur dein allein." (*NS* 655)

There can be little doubt that this monodic mode represents an attempt to rein in sexual passion by means of language. The overt emotional excesses of the very early works are nowhere to be found: there are no longer any references to "Unmaß" or "Übermaß" or to passions "ohne Maß und Ende" (1,5: 454). But the compulsive avoidance of such terms is actually far more suggestive of "Unmaß" than the explicit references to it. Like the characters' ceremonial cleaning and locking, this style is a ritual that affords protection against, yet simultaneously expresses, an obsession with an all-consuming sexual desire. Wildbolz recognises that an essentially sexual dynamic underlies these linguistic rituals when he astutely writes of Stifter's style in *Der Nachsommer*. "Je größer die Leidenschaft, desto mächtiger die rituelle Überformung."[18] The same tendency is even more evident almost ten years after the publication of *Der Nachsommer* in "Der Kuß von Sentze," a story governed by ritual in form as much as in content. Again, the most litaneutic passage of this novella consists of a conversation between the male and female characters, Rupert and Hiltiburg, whose sexual desire for each other appears on the surface of the text to be elided:

> "Hiltiburg, hast du die Schriften gelesen?"
> "Ich habe sie gelesen," antwortete sie.
> "Ich habe sie auch gelesen," sagte ich.
> Dann sprach ich wieder: "Weißt du das Wort?"
> "Ich weiß es," antwortete sie.
> "Ich weiß es auch," sagte ich.
> Dann fragte ich: "Soll ich das Wort sprechen?"
> "Sprich es," antwortete sie. (*GW* III: 711)

Hans-Ulrich Rupp claims of this passage: "Die Wiederholung derselben Worte ist . . . hier aufs innigste vom seelischen Gleichklang der Sprechenden durchdrungen"[19] — but it seems to be far more the case that Stifter employs this style in order to evade the latent sexual exchange that is at once desired and feared. However, as in *Der Nachsommer*, the excess of repetition serves only to draw attention to the very aspect which it attempts to obscure.

In this context, the dialogue in *Witiko* through which the relationship between the hero and Bertha develops merits particular consideration. This novel presents us with the clearest examples of Stifter's tendency towards ritual style in the conversations held between the male and female personae. Tellingly, *Witiko* is unique in that it affords practically no other sexual outlet for the characters. In "Der Kuß von Sentze," for example, passion is allowed fleetingly to rear up in the form of the mysterious, burning kiss that is bestowed upon Rupert as he is about to leave his cousin's house; and in "Der fromme Spruch," the topic of sexuality is explicitly broached when the old Gerlint mistakenly believes the young Gerlint to have designs on her uncle. However, Stifter allows no such passion to ripple the tranquil surface of *Witiko*. The sole contact between the sexes occurs through the dialogue that, conspicuously, never mentions sexuality, although it essentially amounts to prolonged flirtation and foreplay (there can be little doubt that an instant sexual attraction arises between Witiko and Bertha).[20] The ritual in the style of their initial conversation surpasses anything even in *Der Nachsommer* or "Der Kuß von Sentze." Witiko is speaking:

> "Was stehst du mit Deinen Rosen hier da?"
>
> "Ich stehe hier in meiner Heimat da," antwortete das Mädchen; "stehst du auch in derselben, daß du frägst, oder kommst du wo anders her?"
>
> "Ich komme anders woher," sagte der Reiter.
>
> "Wie kannst du dann fragen?" entgegnete das Mädchen.
>
> "Weil ich es wissen möchte," antwortete der Reiter.
>
> "Und wenn ich wissen möchte, was du willst," sagte das Mädchen.
>
> "So würde ich es dir vielleicht sagen," antwortete der Reiter.
>
> "Und ich würde dir vielleicht sagen, warum ich mit den Rosen hier stehe," entgegnete das Mädchen. (5,1: 31)

As their implicit mutual attraction reaches its silent crescendo, the more obsessively does the ritualistic dialogue aim towards a sustained diminuendo until their decision to marry:

> "Ich wollte dich sehen,' sagte Bertha, 'und als ich dich gesehen hatte, warst du mir lieb."
>
> "Und als ich dich gesehen hatte, warst du mir auch lieb," sprach Witiko. "Wir waren zwei Kinder."
>
> "Ja, aber ich habe schöne Ritter und Knaben vor dir gesehen, und keiner war mir lieb," antwortete Bertha.
>
> "Und ich habe schöne Jungfrauen und Mädchen vor dir gesehen, und keine war mir lieb," sagte Witiko.
>
> "Siehst du?" sprach Bertha.

"Und weil ich dir lieb war, hast du mit mir geredet?" fragte Witiko.

"Weil du mir lieb warst, habe ich mit dir geredet," antwortete Bertha.

"Und weil ich dir lieb war, bist du mit mir zu den Sitzsteinen an den Ahornen gegangen?" fragte Witiko.

"Weil du mir lieb warst, bin ich mit dir zu den Sitzsteinen an den Ahornen gegangen," antwortete Bertha.

"Und bist neben mir auf den Steinen gesessen," sagte Witiko.

"Und bin neben dir auf den Steinen gesessen," sprach Bertha.

(5,3: 125–6)

Significantly, the style becomes even more compulsively repetitive once the characters have kissed.[21] It is as if Stifter tries insistently to command with his mode of expression the sensual chaos that the kiss betokens, and as if the more obsessively he structures his use of language, the more threateningly unstructured and manic is the human passion that he feels compelled to control.

"Der fromme Spruch" is perhaps Stifter's only work that bears stylistic comparison with *Witiko*, as suggested in a damning letter of 17 October 1867 to Stifter from Leo Tepe, the editor of *Die katholische Welt*:

Ich schreibe das Mißlingen dieser Erzählung dem *Witiko* zu; denn der Stil des "frommen Spruches" erinnert sehr an den des *Witiko*. Was aber im *Witiko* ansprach und gefiel, berührt hier, in unserm modernen Zeitalter, fremdartig und fast lächerlich. Die unendlichen Zeremonien und hochtrabenden Anreden, welche zwischen Tante, Neffe, Nichte und Oheim gewechselt werden, würden gewiß der Spottlust der Kritiker reichen Stoff bieten. Wir dürfen den frommen Spruch nicht drucken, hauptsächlich Ihretwegen; ich will Ihren literarischen Ruhm nicht verdunkeln helfen.[22]

In this, however, Tepe shows himself quite blind to the fact that the ceremonial dialogue has an essentially human subtext, the conversation between the young male and female characters acting, as in *Witiko*, as a fascinatingly compulsive ritual relating to sexual desire:

"Gerlint," rief Dietwin, "ich kann es nicht ertragen, wenn dein Auge auf irgendeinen Mann blickt."

Gerlint wendete sich um und rief: "Dietwin, ich kann es nicht ertragen, wenn dein Auge auf ein Weib blickt."

"Gerlint," rief Dietwin.

"Dietwin," rief Gerlint. (*FS* 446)

Their passionate kiss abruptly ensues at this point: "Und plötzlich faßten sie sich in die Arme, umschlangen sich und küßten sich auf den

Mund" (a kiss that scarcely justifies Kastner's assertion that we are confronted here by one of "die berühmten Stifterschen Küsse," defined by him as "die liturgischen Friedensküsse, die sich Priester reichen[!]"[23]). Following the kiss, the litany immediately intensifies:

> "Dein Auge blickt auf mich als Gattin, Gerlint," sagte Dietwin.
> "Dein Auge blickt auf mich als Gatte, Dietwin," sprach Gerlint.
> "Ich will dich auf den Händen tragen, Gerlint," sagte Dietwin.
> "Ich werde dir ein treues, gehorsames Weib sein," antwortete Gerlint.
> "Wir werden gemeinsam schalten und wirken," sagte Dietwin.
> "Und nur in der Liebe wetteifern," erwiderte Gerlint.
> "Du hast an dem ersten Tage deines Hierseins die Plätze unserer Kindheit besucht," sagte Dietwin.
> "Du bist auch an diesen Plätzen gewesen," sprach Gerlint.
>
> (*FS* 446–7)

Even now, almost one hundred and thirty years later, Kastner merely complains that such dialogue is unrealistic: "Jeder, der diese Zeilen hört oder liest, weiß, daß lebende Menschen so nicht reden."[24] However, these lines are some of the most eloquent in the whole story and, as Tepe observes in his letter, the same repetitive formality is observed in the exchanges between the young couple's aunt and uncle. This fact has also attracted the attention of critics. Branscombe, for example, states of this style: "Part of Stifter's intention here is surely to highlight the essential sterility of the relationship between brother and sister, which is based on etiquette and family tradition rather than on potentially productive intercourse."[25] However, keeping in mind the observations that I have just made about stylistic repetition, it is quite reasonable to suggest that their dialogue acts as a would-be protection against the illicit sexuality that lies at the unspeakable core of their relationship — but a protection that, like the characters' cleaning and collecting rituals, indulges its sexual driving force by the very act of being so compulsive. These linguistic rituals, then, are closely related to the thematic rituals embodied in the characters' collecting mania in that spontaneous sexual energy is displaced into an absolutely unspontaneous mode of expression. Yet the pent-up, potentially destructive energy underlying the self-control is invariably evident in the tense and extreme moderation of the style.

Notes

[1] Thomas Mann, "Franz Kafka und *Das Schloß*," in Thomas Mann, *Schriften und Reden zur Literatur, Kunst und Philosophie* (Frankfurt am Main: Fischer, 1968), vol. 2, 375.

[2] A fascinating modern analysis of the dialogue in Stifter's fiction (with particular emphasis on the later prose) is offered by Brigid Haines in her monograph *Dialogue and Narrative Design in the Works of Adalbert Stifter* (London: MHRA, 1991).

[3] Matz interprets Stifter's diaries as an attempt at control: "Das System ist von absoluter Perfektion und vollendeter Sinnlosigkeit. Man wird den Eindruck nicht los, daß hier ein Mensch versuchte, wenigstens in der Arithmetik sein Leben unter Kontrolle zu halten" (*Adalbert Stifter*, 317).

[4] This almost pedantic tendency is observed by Peter Branscombe, who recounts an amusing episode in which Stifter corrected Anton Bruckner's grammar ("Some Reflections on the Use of Dialogue in Stifter's Stories," in *Adalbert Stifter heute*, 13).

[5] For technical details about Stifter's use and non-use of commas, see 2,3: 32. The effect of his non-use of commas is that of a mantra, a terrifying (because futile) attempt to fill in the void.

[6] It is fascinating to note here that there is a distinct similarity between Stifter's manic listing and the way in which Keller depicts Züs Bünzlin in his story "Die drei gerechten Kammacher" (The Three Just Comb Makers, 1856). This desiccated (young!) spinster is evoked entirely through her possessions and conversation, both of which disintegrate into chilling lists. She mechanically spouts the names of places: "Rom ist eine große merkwürdige Stadt, allwo der heilige Vater wohnt, und Paris ist eine gar mächtige Stadt mit vielen Seelen und herrlichen Palästen, und in Konstantinopel herrscht der Sultan, von türkischem Glauben, und Lissabon, welches einst durch ein Erdbeben verschüttet ward, ist desto schöner wieder aufgebaut worden. Wien ist die Hauptstadt von Österreich und die Kaiserstadt genannt, und London ist die reichste Stadt der Welt, in Engelland gelegen . . . Petersburg aber ist die Haupt- und Residenzstadt von Rußland, so wie Neapel die Hauptstadt des Königreiches gleichen Namens, mit dem feuerspeienden Berg Vesuvius [a phrase which is itself reminiscent of Stifter]" (Gottfried Keller, *Werke* [Zurich: Hanser, 1965], vol. 4, 226). The list of possessions is even more unsettling: she owns a complete jumble of unrelated things, a meaningless compilation that, as in Stifter's fiction, suggests a terrible underlying chaos: "Sie hatte . . . ein halbes Dutzend silberne Teelöffel, ein Vaterunser mit Gold auf einen roten durchsichtigen Glasstoff gedruckt, den sie Menschenhaut nannte, einen Kirschkern, . . . eine Büchse aus durchbrochenem und mit ro-

tem Taft unterlegten Elfenbein, in welcher ein Spiegelchen war und ein silberner Fingerhut; ferner war darin ein anderer Kirschkern . . . , eine Nuß, worin eine kleine Muttergottes hinter Glas lag, wenn man sie öffnete, ein silbernes Herz, worin ein Riechschwämmchen steckte, und eine Bonbonbüchse aus Zitronenschale, auf deren Deckel eine Erdbeere gemalt war und in welcher eine goldene Stecknadel auf Baumwolle lag, die ein Vergißmeinnicht vorstellte, und ein Medaillon mit einem Monument von Haaren; ferner ein Bündel vergilbter Papiere mit Rezepten und Geheimnissen, ein Fläschchen mit Hoffmannstropfen, ein anderes mit kölnischem Wasser und eine Büchse mit Moschus; eine andere, worin ein Endchen Marderdreck lag, und ein Körbchen, aus wohlriechenden Halmen geflochten, sowie eines aus Glasperlen und Gewürznägelein zusammengesetzt; endlich ein kleines Buch, in himmelblaues geripptes Papier gebunden, mit silbernem Schnitt, betitelt: Goldene Lebensregeln für die Jungfrau als Braut, Gattin und Mutter" (Keller, *Werke*, 213–14).

[7] See also Hans-Ulrich Rupp, *Stifters Sprache* (Zurich: Juris, 1969), in particular his section entitled "Der Spätstil des Dichters," 55–90; H. G. Barnes, "The Function of Conversations and Speeches in *Witiko*," in *German Studies Presented to H. G. Fiedler* (Oxford: Oxford UP, 1938), 1–25; Haines, *Dialogue and Narrative Design*.

[8] Branscombe, "Some Reflections on the Use of Dialogue," 12.

[9] Branscombe, "Some Reflections on the Use of Dialogue," 12.

[10] For a discussion of Stifter's classical tendencies, see Hermann Kunisch, *Adalbert Stifter: Mensch und Wirklichkeit. Studien zu seinem klassischen Stil* (Berlin: Duncker und Humblot, 1950). In his recent biography, Matz argues that "Brigitta," "Der Hagestolz," and "Bergkristall" demonstrate an increasing tendency towards "classical" writing (see in particular his chapter "Bildnis eines Klassikers," *Adalbert Stifter*, 199–217). He is not entirely convinced of the aesthetic value of this style: according to him, "classical perfection" becomes "sterile and pedantic" (211).

[11] Stifter himself refers to his "classical" style in a letter to Heckenast of 25 December 1844 concerning "Die Mappe": "die Erzählung des Obrist muß *graniten* sein, ich glaube, daß diese Episode das erste von mir ist, was man etwa *klassisch* nennen könnte" (*Briefe*, 90; Stifter's emphasis).

[12] J. P. Stern, *Idylls and Realities: Studies in Nineteenth Century German Literature* (London: Methuen, 1971), 109. Dehn makes a similar point. He comments on phrases such as "es ist, wie es ist," with particular emphasis on the later prose, and he argues that this sort of utterance conveys that things necessarily and rightly *are*: "Die Sache ist allein dadurch, daß sie *ist*, gerechtfertigt und sinnvoll. Die Formen von 'sein' sprechen hier geradezu von Notwendigkeit" (*Ding und Vernunft*, 43; his emphasis).

[13] Herbert Seidler, "Die Natur in der Dichtung Stifters," *VASILO*, 17 (1968): 234; his emphasis.

[14] Swales and Swales, *Adalbert Stifter*, 170.

[15] Klatt, "Stifter und das Dämonische," 291.

[16] For a detailed description of Kafka's work for the Workers' Accident Insurance Institute, see Ernst Pawel, *The Nightmare of Reason: A Life of Franz Kafka* (London etc.: Collins Harvil, 1988), 183–93.

[17] The corresponding passage in the journal version reads: "ich habe gesagt, daß es dich reuen würde — ich habe es gesagt" (1,2: 245), which seems to be more typical of "natural" conversation.

[18] Wildbolz, *Langeweile und Faszination*, 113–14.

[19] Rupp, *Stifters Sprache*, 83.

[20] Rupp is passing over central issues when he asserts of this ritual conversation: "Das Einssein der Liebenden wird sprachlich in wunderbarer Weise durch das Mittel der Wiederholung ausgedrückt. Gerade darin, daß die Worte des einen wie ein Echo gleichsam in der Seele des andern widerhallen, liegen Wahrheit und Schönheit dieses Gespräches" (*Stifters Sprache*, 82).

[21] See 5,2: 152.

[22] Fischer, *Leben und Werk*, 657–8.

[23] Jörg Kastner, "Die Liebe im Werk Adalbert Stifters," in *Adalbert Stifter*, ed. Laufhütte and Möseneder, 125.

[24] Kastner, "Die Liebe im Werk Adalbert Stifters," 125.

[25] Branscombe, "Some Reflections on the Use of Dialogue," 20.

4: A Stylistic Dystopia

> "Es ist, wir können sein Nichtsein nicht denken,
> und heißen es in höchster Fülle Gott"
> (Stifter to Heckenast, 12 June 1856)

IN THE PREVIOUS CHAPTER I noted the frequency, obsessiveness even, with which Stifter seeks to transmute the characters' sexual tension and attraction into stylised patterns of dialogue. However, this litaneutical mode of speaking is by no means confined to the sexual sphere: in some ways it is the stylistic heartland of Stifter's later writing. He constantly attempts to uphold the existential security of the personae by repetitively negating catastrophe, but this repetition is disturbing rather than reassuring, and it ultimately conveys the same manic anxiety about existence as the characters' furious piling up of possessions and their frantic rituals of locking doors and erecting barriers.

"Der fromme Spruch" is perhaps the best place to start, as its minimal "action" consists almost solely of stylistic repetition. Stifter described it as "eine meiner edelsten und lebensvollsten Dichtungen,"[1] but, as Tepe's letter indicates, the story was poorly received by the editorial board of *Die katholische Welt*, the journal to which it was submitted for publication, and still attracts little critical interest today.[2] The letter of 17 October 1867 in which Tepe explains and defends the board's refusal to publish it, opens thus:

> Ich fürchte Ihnen wehe zu tun, ich zögerte lange und zog meine Freunde zu Rate, aber länger darf ich nicht zaudern und ich muß Ihnen offen gestehen, daß "Der fromme Spruch" keinen Beifall gefunden hat . . . Man wollte anfangs gar nicht glauben, daß die Erzählung aus Ihrer Feder stammte . . . Man wollte den Schluß nicht einmal lesen, man fand das Ganze zu langweilig . . . Nun kurz die Gründe: "Die Erzählung ist unnatürlich; solche steife Personen gibt es nicht, ihre Reden sind alle wie auf Schrauben gestellt; die alltäglichen Dinge sind in endloser Breitspurigkeit vorgeführt; die Handlung ist fast null, der Stil ist gezwungen und voll Wiederholungen; man glaubt kaum, daß es dem Verfasser ernst ist, und man ist manchmal geneigt, das Ganze für eine Karikatur der aristokratischen Familien zu halten."[3]

In his reply, Stifter clutches at the straw offered to him by Tepe, and makes a belated attempt to justify the story in terms of humour, a statement that has all too frequently been taken at face value[4]:

> Es sollte allerdings die Lächerlichkeit nicht des hohen Adels, dessen Benehmen bei uns durchgängig leicht und fein ist, sondern gewisser Leute auf dem Lande mit veralteten Formen nicht gerade satirisch sondern scherzend dargestellt werden.[5]

To my mind, Stifter's statement is of little use in helping us to explain the effectiveness of the story — for indeed it *is* a supremely effective story. The true power and fascination of the work lie, rather, in the very elements Tepe found distasteful: in the "contrived" and "repetitive" style that, far from being "too tedious," reveals nothing so much as pathological anxiety, the fear of the void.[6]

This is most clearly recorded in the style of the exchanges that take place between the uncle and aunt. As we have seen, the two characters' ritualistic conversation partly pertains to sexuality and self-control. Here, though, Stifter presents us with phatic conversation that testifies not just to the security gained from the control of passionate urges, but to a mutual *existential* security. This is well demonstrated by the ceremonial formulae traditionally recited by Dietwin and Gerlint when they meet to parley at their yearly "Frühlingsreichstag" (*FS* 387) — formulae that serve only to exchange information they both already know. Such repetition shows "Der fromme Spruch" to provide a linguistic expression of the characters' actions in *Der Nachsommer* of which Heinrich reports: "Man wiederholte vielleicht oft gesagte Worte, man zeigte sich manches, das man schon oft gesehen hatte, und machte sich auf Dinge aufmerksam, die man ohnehin kannte" (*NS* 369). It is this repetitive style that, on the surface, allows the characters ritually to confirm to one another and to themselves that their existences are secure. Dietwin and Gerlint are allowed to breathe a sigh of sublime relief that nothing has happened since the last time they spoke the formula; they feel able to rest in the knowledge that the crisis has been averted for another year:

> "Ist kein Unfall vorgekommen?" fragte sie.
> "Ein zerbrochenes Rad, das wieder gemacht worden ist," entgegnete er, "eine kranke Kuh, die wieder gesund ist, und anderes, dessen ich mich nicht mehr entsinne."
> "Das ist ohne Bedeutung," sagte sie, "bei mir ist gar nichts vorgekommen."
> "So stehen die Sachen vortrefflich," antwortete er.
> "Es geht so gut, wie alles nur immer gehen kann," sagte sie, "und so sei noch einmal gegrüßt, Dietwin."
> "Sei gegrüßt, Gerlint," antwortete er. (*FS* 372)

The events to which Dietwin alludes are so insignificant that they are easily folded into the comforting blanket of "gar nichts." Yet the threat remains, in that the repetition has the effect of drawing attention to the anxiety from which it apparently tries to detract, rather than to the surety it purports to maintain. A similarly anxious confirmation of present and future security is intimated by the manner in which one character formulaically reiterates — and thus affirms the validity of — the words uttered by the previous character. Such a ritual introduces the aunt and uncle to the reader:

> "Das Heil Gottes, Gerlint," sagte er, "und möge dir dieser Tag noch recht oft wiederkehren."
> "Das Heil Gottes, Dietwin," sagte sie, "und möge dir dieser Tag noch recht oft wiederkehren." (*FS* 373)

This mode intensifies as the story progresses, climaxing in the arrestingly, almost absurdly, repetitive circumlocution that takes place between the two characters:

> "Lieber Bruder," sagte die Tante, "es muß doch einmal von dem geredet werden, wovon geredet werden muß."
> "So rede, liebe Gerlint," antwortete der Oheim, "wovon, wie du meinst, geredet werden muß." . . .
> Darauf sprach der Oheim: "'Ja, es muß von dem geredet werden, wovon geredet werden muß." (*FS* 435–6)

Rupp sees this iterative dialogue as "ein Mittel, um das gegenseitige Verständnis und die Gleichgesinntheit Dietwins und Gerlints sprachlich zum Ausdruck zu bringen,"[7] but this kind of comment does not even begin to meet the challenge posed by such a style. Matz likewise fails to recognise any subtext when he claims: "Im *Frommen Spruch* gibt es Szenen, die zur reinen Tautologie werden, zur Bedeutungslosigkeit als Stilprinzip."[8] Far from indulging in meaningless tautology, Stifter is deploying style as a final bastion against the unknown, the unpredictable, the unsaid, in his characters' lives. Like the countless high walls, iron grilles and other barriers figured in his stories, it represents an attempt to assuage a terrible fear, as exemplified in characters such as Abdias and the *Hagestolz*. This is the feature Klatt recognises when he writes that Stifter's excessively calm language is the result of desperation rather than conviction, his "letzter geistiger Halt, wo alles andere versagt,"[9] and the one to which Lunding alludes when he asks: "Wird es Stifter gelingen, durch die Magie der Form die beglückende existentielle Beruhigung zu erreichen?"[10] The refrain effect in the above exchange, for example, is so relentless that there is little choice but to infer that Stifter is motivated by fear rather than by faith — after all, he himself

wrote to Heckenast of his "gegenstandlose Angst" (*MSB* 843). The terror of the slip of the tongue that could explode the specious wholeness of the existences he so painstakingly builds up for his characters urges him with increasing relentlessness to exercise absolute control over the words that they speak. The dialogue, for instance, reaches almost operatic proportions when the younger Dietwin expresses his fear that his aunt might act against his wishes, and reassurance is gained only when Stifter makes her repeat his words:

> "Tante, Tante, Tante, diese Puppen, nie, nie, nie. Ich werde zu keiner Puppe herabsteigen . . . und ich bitte dich, Tante, rede nicht davon, ich bitte dich, rede nicht davon." Ich erwiderte: "Nun, ich rede nicht davon." (*FS* 440)

Yet just as the repeated actions or "Sitten" of the characters cannot intimate unequivocal "Sittlichkeit," so too the linguistic repetitions cannot promise that man's dread is groundless. Stifter's own irrational, obsessive fear of catastrophe and of sudden extinction without rhyme or reason is clearly evident in the exchange he records in his essay "Aus dem Bayrischen Walde" (From the Bavarian Forest, 1868):

> "Martin," sagte ich [i.e. Stifter himself], "wenn uns ein Schlitten begegnet."
> "Es begegnet uns keiner," antwortete er.
> "Wenn uns aber doch einer begegnet," sagte ich wieder.
> "Es begegnet uns keiner," antwortete er.
> "Wenn uns aber doch einer begegnet," beharrte ich.
> "Dann weiß ich es nicht," sagte er.
> Es begegnete uns aber keiner. (*MSB* 591)

This proto-Kafkaesque conversation affords us one of the most superb examples of Stifter's litaneutical mode that, in its very excess of securely controlled repetition, points to a subtext of unassuageable fear.[11] This is the hidden dimension that T. J. Reed perceived when he elegantly stated of *Der Nachsommer*: "the worthy occupations seem brittle, their motives anxiety rather than harmony. Stifter's unruffled repetitions start to seem a slow-motion hysteria"[12]; and it is a feature of which Theodor Adorno showed his awareness when he wrote: "Die letzten Novellen Stifters geben vom Übergang der gegenständlichen Treue in die manische Obsession die deutlichste Kunde."[13]

Stifter's unique, "manically obsessive" literary style, then, records the individual characters' fears of the fragility inherent in their existences. However, it would be a mistake to view stylistic repetition only in relation to single characters. More significantly, it suggests a threat that transcends the human sphere and encompasses a metaphysical vista

of terrifying meaninglessness. This may, on an initial impression, seem implausible; it may be tempting simply to agree with Tepe and dismiss Stifter's repetitive style as "tedious." Yet if this really were the case, how could Thomas Mann come to the conclusion that this same style brings about a "Sensationellwerden der Langenweile" that is "im schönsten Sinne unheimlich?"[14] It appears that Mann was far more sensitive than most early readers of Stifter to the subtext of metaphysical chaos that makes the rhythm of repetition so eerily compelling. I suggested earlier that the increasingly litaneutical mode Stifter employs is partly related to a kind of classicising process and partly connected with an ethos of control. However, more crucial is the fact that the descriptive paragraphs and the passages of dialogue both present the reader with a kind of Minimalism — but one that is uniquely Stifterian in that it goes hand in hand with a kind of furious aggregation. His essays work in exactly the same way. "Winterbriefe aus Kirchschlag" (Winter Letters from Kirchschlag, 1866) is a case in point: its obsessive list of temperature changes is a prime instance of the "encyclopaedic enumeration of data" that Stern sees as one of the characteristic features of Stifter's writing.[15] He claims that it "leaves the reader gasping for air,"[16] but to my mind "breathtaking" would be a more apt metaphor: once we recognise the underlying dread, this prose has a compelling and awesome force:

> Ich verzeichne an dieser Stelle mehrere Wärmebeobachtungen, die ich im Monate Jänner auf einem 80gradigen Thermometer, der sich gegen Süden außerhalb eines Fensters befindet, in der Sonne um 12 Uhr machte. Am 7. 18°, am 15. 23°, am 19. 24°, am 20. 20°, am 21. 19°, am 22. 21°, am 27. 19°, am 28. 21½°. An diesen Tagen sahen wir auf dem Donautale unbeweglichen dicken Nebel liegen. Es mögen noch einige Mittags-Wärmebeobachtungen von trüben Tagen, welche einzelne Sonnenblicke hatten, folgen: Am 9. 8½°, am 11. 6°, am 16. 7°, am 23. 6°, am 24. 5°, am 29. 7°. Zum Schlusse führe ich Mittag-Beobachtungen bei Schneefällen an: Am 8. 1°, am 10. 0°, am 12. -0.2°, am 30. 2° . . . Genaueres [!] wird sich ergeben. (*MSB* 525)[17]

This is a style that flies directly in the face of the nineteenth-century trends of Realism and Naturalism whilst seeming to embrace them, and what is unsettling, even menacing, about it is that the whole mode comes across as obsessive in its studied monotony. Again, Thomas Mann was clearly sensible of this when he named Stifter "einen der größten und ermutigendsten Ehrenretter der Langenweile,"[18] and spoke of the profound "Hintergründigkeit" of his apparently Apollonian style. This is absolutely not the comforting monotony of "die gewöhnlichen alltäglichen in Unzahl wiederkehrenden Handlungen der

Menschen" extolled by Stifter in the *Bunte Steine* Preface (2,2: 14), nor is it, as Martin Swales would have it, simply "ein Prosastil von einer geradezu absurden Pedanterie."[19] It is a wholly threatening mode, and awareness of it is essential to an understanding of Stifter, for it is in this manner that the most severely dystopian aspect of his complex vision is revealed. *This* is what Tepe, unsurprisingly, failed to realise when he dismissed "Der fromme Spruch" as "tedious"; *this* is what one contemporary reviewer could not recognise when he wrote:

> der ... *Fromme Spruch* ... ist unerträglich langweilig. Auf vierundsechzig enggedruckten Seiten das triviale Thema: "Ich heirate, du heiratest, er heiratet, wir heiraten" usw. von ganz gewöhnlichen, in keiner Weise originell gezeichneten Menschen abgehandelt und dabei das Ende bereits auf den ersten Seiten mit Bestimmtheit vorauszusehen, ist eine harte Zumutung.[20]

The same "tone-deafness" would also seem to account for Johann Aprent's attempts to make the story more palatable for the reader by bowdlerising it with verbal variations when he published it after Stifter's death.[21]

The power of Stifter's narrative lies to no small extent in its deliberate monotony; in the insistent patterns of tone and rhythm that make his work so disturbing. The process is already wonderfully evident in "Turmalin," for example, where the mode of presentation makes the picture of the infant both perfectly iconic and desperately fragile:

> Unter diesem Zelte stand auf einem Tische ein feiner Korb, in dem Korbe war ein weißes Bettchen, und in dem Bettchen war das Kind der beiden Eheleute, das Mädchen, bei dem sie öfter standen, und die winzigen rothen Lippen und die rosigen Wangen und die geschlossenen Äuglein betrachteten. (2,2: 139)

A similar accumulation of apparently blissful diminutives and fairytale-style repetition is displayed by the story "Kazensilber" (Mica, 1853):

> Die Großmutter ... dekte ... ein weißes Tuch über das Tischlein, ... sie legte an jedem Size ein Tellerchen auf das Tischlein, sie that auf das Tellerchen ebenfalls ein weißes Tüchlein, und legte ein Löffelchen Messerlein und Gabel zu jedem Teller. Dann that sie aus der Flasche Milch in das Milchtöpflein. (2,2: 290)

> Die Mutter hatte früher auf alle Pläze der Kinder an dem Tische Tellerchen legen lassen. Sie ging zu dem Tellerchen Blondköpfchens, that mit einem Löffel Erdbeeren auf dasselbe, und Blondköpfchen begann zu essen. Sie ging zu dem Tellerchen Schwarzköpfchens, that Erdbeeren darauf, und Schwarzköpfchen fing an zu essen. Sie ging zu dem Tellerchen Braunköpfchens, that Erdbeeren darauf, und Braun-

köpfchen aß sie. Sie ging zu dem Tellerchen des braunen Mädchens, legte Erdbeeren darauf, und das braune Mädchen begann zu essen. Dann ging sie wieder zur Thür hinaus. Ein anderes Mal kam sie wieder, war wieder ein Schwarzköpfchen, brachte allerlei Dinge, und war unter den Kindern. (2,2: 291)

Both of these examples demonstrate Stifter employing all the classic signals that indicate solid, calm, idyllic perfection. Here and elsewhere, he uses iconically "safe" personae, fairytale language and rhythms, and emblematic details connoting purity, untouchedness and untouchability, in order to build up a tableau that initially seems paradisiacal — but which, like the characters' collections, tips over into mania precisely by being rendered as it were top-heavy with perfection. The crucial point here is that mania is not just hidden away below a measured, moderate surface: the more moderate the surface seems, the more manic the depths actually are. And the more the reader becomes attuned to this style, the more rapidly one recognises the tell-tale signs of this hidden menace, this sense of disaster waiting to happen. With this in mind, it may be tempting to agree with Natalie when she ominously pronounces in *Der Nachsommer*: "Alles ist so schön, daß es fast zu schön ist" (*NS* 493).

But what constitutes the menace that this style covertly reveals? As suggested earlier, it is connected with man's imperfect reason and with the distant rumbling of chaotic passion. More threateningly, though, it transcends man's boundaries and relates to existence beyond the human dimension. In Chapter Three I used a passage from "Granit" to exemplify the apparent faith in the inherent meaning of "things" that informs the repetend "sein." However, particularly in the later works, the same mode reverberates with obsession in its repetition and highly-charged rhythms. This is the case in the doctor's description of his native forest in the *Letzte Mappe*, for example, in which the emphasis placed on the verb "sein" is too marked to be convincing:

Da ist Wald und Wald und Wald. In demselben sind Föhren, Fichten, Tannen, Buchen und Birken in Menge. Alle andern Bäume und Gesträuche sind auch da. Dann sind rauschende Wässer und graue Steine. Dann sind hellgrüne Wiesenflächen und verschiedenfarbige Felder. Dann sind braune Holzhäuser mit Steinen auf dem Dache und glänzenden Fenstern, dann sind weiße Kirchtürme und lustige Marktflecken. (*MSB* 85–6)

For Wildbolz this is mere "banalisation," part of the "collapse into manneredness and triviality" that he discerns in the *Letzte Mappe* as a whole.[22] But this is a decidedly mistaken view. The more urgently Stifter uses "sein" to intimate divine essence embodied in these objects, the

more insistently he draws attention to a terrifying absence of any intrinsic meaning, to that "letzte Unvernunft des Seins" invoked and ostensibly discarded in "Abdias" (1,5: 238). The passage above delivers an example of what one might call a "secular litany," one in which God is no longer present. In a letter to Heckenast of 12 June 1856, Stifter's own ultimate lack of belief in indestructible essence pervades the peculiar logic by means of which he desperately tries to sustain it. We again notice the way in which he uses "sein" in a dubious attempt to convey a sense of the "essence of things" when he writes: "Es *ist*, wir können sein Nichtsein nicht denken, und heißen es in höchster Fülle Gott" (*MSB* 748; Stifter's emphasis).[23]

What Stifter presents us with is a seeming picture of thereness — but with crucial parts of it as it were screamingly blanked out, creating not a sense of completeness or objectivity, but a profound sense of enigma. Matz, despite perceiving much of Stifter's modern appeal, fails to see the overwhelmingly modernist elements in the *Letzte Mappe*. He describes the language here as a "Rückkehr . . . zu einer sprachlichen Form, die vor den hermetischen Experimenten der Spätzeit liegt."[24] But he is entirely mistaken. Take, for example, the conversation in which Anna repeatedly tells Innozenz why she must refuse his proposal of marriage:

> "Jetzt noch nicht."
> Wir waren erstaunt, Innozenz war fast bestürzt, und sagte: "Anna, hast du mir denn nicht erst vor kurzer Zeit gesagt, daß du nie einen andern Mann zum Gatten haben willst als mich?"
> "Innozenz," antwortete sie, "jetzt noch nicht. Ja, ich habe es gesagt. Innozenz, jetzt noch nicht."
> Der Vater fragte: "Aber wann denn, Anna?"
> "Jetzt noch nicht, Vater," antwortete sie wieder.
> "Habe ich dir etwas zu Leide getan, Anna?" fragte Innozenz mit einem schmerzlichen Angesichte.
> "Nein, Innozenz," erwiderte sie, "du bist recht gut, und ich liebe dich aus meiner treuen Seele." . . .
> "Ich will ja nichts erzwingen," sagte Innozenz, "ich habe mich nur geirrt."
> "Nein, du hast dich nicht geirrt," sagte Anna, "es wird schon werden." (*MSB* 214)

This insistent repetition strives to convince us that we are being offered a full and plausible explanation. Yet for all its insistence, the actual words bear no explicatory power; we may agree with Mathilde when she sceptically declares in *Der Nachsommer*: "Ja, ja, das sind die Worte" (*NS* 668), or with the narrator of "Prokopus," who despairs: "Was das

Wort bedeuten mochte, kann man nicht enträtseln" (*GW* III: 562). Rupp interprets this conversation as an example of the spiritual connection between Anna and Augustinus:

> Die seelische Gleichgestimmtheit der Geschwister und ihre überaus zarte gegenseitige Rücksichtnahme erfahren hier in Worten und Gebärden den vollkommenen Ausdruck.[25]

This, though, seems wholly to miss the point, namely the impossibility of communicating any kind of real meaning. The first conversation Augustinus has with Margarita after she has declined his proposal suggests this just as strongly:

> "Sprecht, lieber Freund," antwortete sie, "setzet Euch zu mir auf diesen kleinen Stuhl, und sprecht alle Worte, die Euch gut dünken, und die Euerm Herzen zu einer Erleichterung sein können."
> "Wie kann ich sprechen, wenn das Ziel des Gespräches weggenommen ist," entgegnete ich.
> "Sprecht außerhalb dieses Zieles," sagte sie.
> "Gibt es da etwas?" fragte ich.
> "Ich fühle, daß es noch sehr viel gibt," antwortete sie.
> "Ihr fühlt das?" fragte ich.
> "Ja," entgegnete sie. (*MSB* 156)

Such stylistic repetition may on one level appear to fill in the gaps but, in effect, it opens up much larger ones. Stifter tries with the incantatory quality of his language to persuade us that wholeness is apodictical, but his repetitions serve only to highlight the void since they are unable to confer philosophical validity on objects or to bridge the gaps in his logic. We are ultimately left with the abysmal, absurd chaos of meaninglessness where wholeness and cohesion, along with God, have ceased to exist. Seen in this light, the texts not only illustrate the disturbing realisation that man's reason may not be the key that unlocks the door to the universe; they demonstrate the far more devastating insight that there is in one sense no universe for him to access. In this respect, the *Letzte Mappe* is again all-important. The conversation in which Augustinus advises a villager to consult the doctor (i.e. Augustinus himself) again shows how Stifter's style anticipates Kafka's or even Beckett's:

> "So fragt den neuen Doktor, welcher in der Gegend ist," sagte ich.
> "Ach der Doktor," antwortete er, "wer wird denn zu dem Doktor gehen?"
> "Warum denn nicht?" fragte ich.
> "Ach nein," sagte er, und schüttelte den Kopf.
> "Aber einen Grund müßt ihr doch haben," sagte ich.
> "Der Grund ist, daß wir nicht zu dem Doktor gehen," sagte er.

"Nun, so geht nicht zu dem Doktor," sprach ich.

"Ja, ja, da habt ihr recht," antwortete er, "wir gehen nicht zum Doktor." (*MSB* 67)

It is this conversation that provokes Martin and Erika Swales to comment: "the very style that we have come to associate with Stifter ceases to be the organ of Reason and instead articulates an absurd, inconsequential world."[26] However, their point can be taken still further: Stifter's later fiction is twentieth-century Absurdism before the twentieth century. The *Letzte Mappe* in particular is constantly poised on the brink of the absurd: Augustinus, for instance, echoes Stephan's declaration of hate in "Brigitta" to far more absurd effect:

"Das ist ja ganz unaussprechlich, das ist unaussprechlich," rief er. "Eustachius! Eustachius! Wo wird er denn jetzt sein, und wo wird er denn sein!" (*MSB* 50)

Witiko similarly demonstrates the extent to which Stifter's fiction is Absurdism *avant la lettre*: here, actions are "explained" in the same manner as the villager "explains" his aversion to doctors: "Ich frage, weil ich frage," states Thiemo von der Aue; "Und ich gehe, weil ich gehe," rejoins Witiko (5,2: 236). In this context, it is significant that the style of the conversation in the *Letzte Mappe* also suggests the frailness of identity, as Brigid Haines compellingly argues.[27] The villager not only fails to communicate his reasons for refusing medical treatment, but, in the very absoluteness of his rejection of the doctor, he tears off Augustinus's mask, laconically negating the "identity" that the character has carved out for himself.

This later prose transports us fully into the zone of the Absurd — and this is what makes Stifter a truly radical writer. He constantly seeks to bridge the abyss, but his obsessive attempts to do so only express all the more vividly its true magnitude. His medium is his actual message: he presents us with realms of mania, with a linguistic dystopia, the stylistic equivalent of the otherness envisioned in, for example, the uncle's island in "Der Hagestolz." The repetition by means of which he insistently seeks to maintain an orderly sense of positivity takes us into the unspeakable un-place of the negative, into a chaotic *Nichts*. The threat underlying repeated affirmation is perhaps most persuasively illustrated by a comparison between "Granit" and "Bergkristall." In the former, the little boy's litany of "Ja Großvater" (2,2: 32–5) is, broadly speaking, an act of faith, an affirmative used to confirm the inherent meaning of his God-given surroundings. In the latter, though, Sanna's litany of utter faith and trust in Man (personified in her brother) helps to carry her into a sphere that is in effect *beyond* humanity and *beyond* divinity

("hier war nichts zu verkündigen," 2,2: 227). Her "Ja Konrad" is an act of misplaced faith; her excessive positivity confirms a negative. Again, the changes made to the story are revealing. Sanna is made to reiterate "Ja Konrad" seventeen times in the book version, as opposed to only three times in the journal version.[28] However, it is the designed monotony of her utterance in the later version that makes this so much more chilling than the earlier one. Each "Ja Konrad" acts as an uncannily measured step further into the chaotic, godless wasteland of the mountain, into the realm of the "Nichts." Not only have the children been transported to an alien dimension; Stifter's style, too, takes us beyond the pale, into the screamingly silent zones of unspeakable, even unthinkable, otherness.

Notes

[1] Letter to Tepe of 12 March 1867, cited in Ruthilde Frischenschlager, "Über Editionsschwierigkeiten des *Frommen Spruches*," *VASILO*, 19 (1970): 11.

[2] The most interesting of the very few modern critical analyses are as follows: Swales and Swales, *Adalbert Stifter*, 165–70; Albrecht Koschorke and Andreas Ammer, "Der Text ohne Bedeutung oder die Erstarrung der Angst: Zu Stifters letzter Erzählung *Der fromme Spruch*," *Deutsche Vierteljahresschrift für Literaturwissenschaft und Geistesgeschichte*, 61 (1987): 676–719; and Matz, *Adalbert Stifter*, 382.

[3] Letter to Stifter of 12 October 1867, cited in Fischer, *Leben und Werk*, 656–7. A review by Tepe in the *Westfälischer Mercur* expressed similar views (see Enzinger, *Stifter im Urteil seiner Zeit*, 344).

[4] Wildbolz sees the formal style of the work in terms of "lovable irony" (*Langeweile und Faszination*, 129), whilst Branscombe states that the cliché "Ehen werden in dem Himmel geschlossen" is "endlessly and wittily varied" ("Some Reflections on the Use of Dialogue," 20). However, Swales and Swales are probably nearer the mark when they fail to find any deliberate irony in the story ("We find it impossible to perceive any traces of irony in the stories [*Der Kuß von Sentze* and *Der fromme Spruch*]," *Adalbert Stifter*, 169).

[5] Letter to Tepe of 31 October 1867, cited in Fischer, *Leben und Werk*, 658.

[6] Erik Lunding is one of the few critics to perceive the hidden fear in this style, when he characterises "Der fromme Spruch" and "Der Kuß von Sentze" as "die beiden merkwürdigsten Erzeugnisse deutscher Erzählkunst im vorigen Jahrhundert" (*Adalbert Stifter: Mit einem Anhang über Kierkegaard und die existentielle Wissenschaft* [Copenhagen: Nyt Nordisk

Forlag Arnold Busck, 1946], 109). Matz, for his part, sees the "modernism" of "Der fromme Spruch": "Mit dieser Minimalkunst . . . , wagte sich Stifter weiter in die Moderne vor, als ihm auch Freunde folgen mochten" (*Adalbert Stifter*, 383).

[7] Rupp, *Stifters Sprache*, 83.

[8] Matz, *Adalbert Stifter*, 382.

[9] Klatt, "Stifter und das Dämonische," 291.

[10] Lunding, *Adalbert Stifter*, 97.

[11] This text also provides us with one of the most revealing examples of Stifter's obsessive fears regarding his health.

[12] T. J. Reed, "The *Goethezeit* and its Aftermath," in *Germany: A Companion to German Studies*, ed. Malcolm Pasley (London: Methuen, 1972), 534–5.

[13] T. W. Adorno, "Über epische Naivetät," in T. W. Adorno, *Noten zur Literatur* (Frankfurt am Main: Suhrkamp, 1958), vol. 1, 56.

[14] Mann, *Briefe*, 458–9.

[15] Stern, *Reinterpretations*, 251.

[16] Stern, *Reinterpretations*, 251.

[17] Similarly obsessive detail characterises the essay "Über den geschnitzten Hochaltar in der Kirche zur Kefermarkt" (On the Carved High Altar in Kefermarkt Church, *GW VI*: 467–83).

[18] Mann, *Briefe*, 458.

[19] Martin Swales, "Litanei und Leerstelle: Zur Modernität Adalbert Stifters," *VASILO*, 36 (1987), 3/4: 80.

[20] Cited in Enzinger, *Stifter im Urteil seiner Zeit*, 354.

[21] In a letter to Heckenast, Aprent admits: "Jetzt ist nicht mehr zu unterscheiden, ob der Strich von Stifter oder von mir herrührt" (cited in Moriz Enzinger, *Gesammelte Aufsätze zu Adalbert Stifter* [Vienna: Österreichische Verlagsanstalt, 1967], 26). It has been very difficult for editors to agree on what the "original" version of the story might have been — and this is perhaps one reason why it was not published until 1960. It first appeared in the so-called *Prag-Reichenberger Ausgabe* (*Säm(m)tliche Werke*, ed. Sauer, Hüller, Eben, and Wilhelm. Prague: J. G. Calve; Reichenberg: Franz Kraus; Graz: Stiasnh, 1901–60, vol. 13); Aprent's version is still much more widely available than Stifter's own.

[22] Wildbolz, *Langeweile und Faszination*, 140.

[23] Earlier in the same letter, the same fears are evident: "Wie es sein wird, wenn wir die Grenze dieses Lebens betreten haben, wenn sein letzter Atemzug vorbei ist — wer kann es sagen? Daß alles, was göttlich ist, nicht untergehen kann, ist gewiß: geht doch nicht einmal ein Sandkorn verloren

nicht einmal ein Wassertropfen, wir wissen es und wir sehen es, daß beides nicht *Nichts* werden könne" (*MSB* 747; Stifter's emphasis). Stifter's views in this letter are strikingly similar to the way Büchner sees Spinoza's and Descartes' supposed proofs of God. Spinoza, according to Büchner, arbitrarily deifies his notion of "eine ewige und unendliche Wesenheit" (Georg Büchner, *Sämtliche Werke und Briefe: Historisch-kritische Gesamtausgabe*, ed. Lehmann [Munich: Hanser, 1974], vol. 2, 239) and, by doing so, abandons philosophy ("Hier hört der Philosoph auf und er vergöttert willkührlich das, was in sich und worin Alles ist," 240; this could easily apply to Stifter). Likewise, what Büchner has to say about Descartes' God could easily be said of Stifter's God. According to Büchner, he fills the void; he is a bridge over the abyss or a ladder out of it: "Gott ist es, der den Abgrund zwischen Denken und Erkennen, zwischen Subject und Object ausfüllt, er ist die Brücke zwischen dem *cogito ergo sum*, zwischen dem einsamen, irren, nur einem, dem Selbstbewußtseyn, gewissen, Denken und der Außenwelt. Der Versuch ist etwas naiv ausgefallen, aber man sieht doch, wie instinctartig scharf schon Cartesius das Grab der Philosophie abmaß; sonderbar ist es freilich wie er den lieben Gott als Leiter gebrauchte, um herauszukriechen" (153). This is God as a desperate last resort, as a "lifeline" ("Es blieb ihm [Descartes] also um sich aus dem Abgrund seines Zweifels zu retten nur ein Strick, an den er sein ganzes System hängte und hakte, *Gott*," 155; Büchner's emphasis).

[24] Matz, *Adalbert Stifter*, 385.

[25] Rupp, *Stifters Sprache*, 87.

[26] Swales and Swales, *Adalbert Stifter*, 132.

[27] Haines, *Dialogue and Narrative Design*, 130.

[28] Compare 2,2: 219–34 with 2,1: 156–65.

5: *Witiko* and the Blighted Paradise

"Alles ist so schön, daß es fast zu schön ist"
(*Der Nachsommer*)

TRADITIONALLY, EVEN THE MOST ADMIRING of Stifter's interpreters have tended to fight shy of *Witiko*.[1] This is a curious and regrettable state of affairs, given that this work undoubtedly represents his most singular achievement; indeed I would define it as his manic masterpiece. Whilst *Bunte Steine* and the early *Studien*, for example, are clearly indebted to influences such as Goethe and Jean Paul, *Witiko* bears little or no resemblance to the literary works of any other author.[2] This has been variously commented upon by critics such as Matz, who claims:

> Im 19. Jahrhundert ist Stifters Buch wahrscheinlich der am radikalsten unzeitgemäße Roman der gesamten deutschsprachigen Literatur, und im Gegensatz zum Willen seines Autors hat er Bestand nicht als politisch-historischer Entwurf, sondern als einzigartiges ästhetisches Wagnis, als Sprachkunstwerk und stilistisches Experiment.[3]

Lunding rightly calls the novel "diese ohne Zweifel sonderbarste Dichtung der deutschen Prosa im 19. Jahrhundert"[4]; Heinz Otto Burger believes that its *unzeitgemäß* quality makes it comparable only to Büchner's *Woyzeck*[5]; Klatt remarks that the later fiction in general is comparable with nothing else in German literature.[6] Fellow writers, too, have seen it in similar terms: for Hermann Hesse and Thomas Mann it was nothing less than "unique"[7] and "incomparable."[8]

There can be little doubt that the most arresting feature of *Witiko* in stylistic terms is that it is written almost entirely in the litaneutical mode that I have shown to be increasingly characteristic of Stifter — "litany" being perhaps the most apposite term for Stifter's style, as it implies incantation and repetition, not to mention the sacral and supplicatory, all of which are central to his genius. As I have already mentioned, deliberate monotony is by no means a feature exclusive to *Witiko*, but it certainly reaches its apogee in this, Stifter's final completed work. It is this prose style that has received both praise and condemnation: whilst Hesse lauds its "langsamer, würdiger, prachtvoll uneiliger Schritt,"[9] Stern simply states that it "ceases to be readable."[10] Astute though many of Stifter's admirers (and disparagers) undoubtedly are, none of them

really succeeds in penetrating the disturbing depths that lie within his narrative mode. Hesse appears to be on the right lines when he claims that Stifter is "modern, aufregend und vorbildlich,"[11] but he ultimately, and to my mind mistakenly, relates Stifter's modernity to his ethos of "Ehrfurcht."[12] Similarly, H. G. Barnes is correct in warning us not to dismiss *Witiko* as "intolerably prolix," but his reasons for this are based on an implicit and unquestioning acceptance of the "sanftes Gesez"[13] — a stance also shared by Franz Hüller.[14]

Enticing though it may be to dismiss such comments out of hand, it is nonetheless necessary to consider how such opinions could have arisen. On the face of it *Witiko* appears to display a supreme faith in reason even more unequivocally than the other works so far discussed, as well as the irrefragability of both a satisfying morality and a divinely or-dained universe. The content and style of this towering novel are structured around ceremonial repetition in a way that far exceeds any of Stifter's other works — and in a way that appears to suggest more strongly than ever the incontrovertibility of reason and the serene world order of "das Alltägliche" extolled twelve years previously in the *Bunte Steine* preface. Thus we witness the tradition observed by Witiko and his countrymen of salting their bread before eating it (5,1: 216); we hear that Witiko always tends his own horse (5,1: 103, 216); we are told that certain formalities are observed at the end of every battle (5,3: 335); and the customary exchange of gifts is executed in a ceremonial manner which surpasses even that of *Der Nachsommer* (5,3: 201). The same gentle law of reason appears to prevail in Stifter's implication that all events can be categorised into neat packages of unambiguous lin-guistic formulae for the reader to receive happily and unquestioningly. This tendency is evident, for instance, in an exchange between Wentila and Agnes, in which the actions referred to are instantly rolled up into tidy little capsules labelled "christian duty":

> "Meine Mutter hat nur eine Christenpflicht geübt," sagte die Mutter Witiko's.
> "Und mein Dank ist auch nur eine Christenpflicht gewesen," antwortete Agnes. (5,2: 216)

More broadly, one of the main themes of the novel concerns the appointment of the duke. However, in keeping with the sublime sense of reasonable order that characterises the surface of the novel, the cru-cial issue is not who should succeed to the dukedom, but by which law the successor should be determined. The role of man is secondary to that of the ritual, as is made graphically clear through the words which Stifter places in Bolemil's mouth at the assembly: "Nicht die Frage ist

jetzt die größte, wer soll Herzog sein, sondern die, wie soll die Nach-
folge bestellt werden?" (5,1: 142).[15] The same ordering principle of reason is indicated by the way that words are uttered and then echoed at
the formal meetings:

> Der Bischof Zdik . . . rief . . . "ich verwarne dich, Milhost, daß du
> die Ordnung der Versammlung nicht störst."
> "Die Ordnung, die Ordnung," riefen mehrere Stimmen.
> (5,1: 126)

There can be little doubt that controlled dialogue such as this functions
partly as an expression of man's capacity to impose his will on the world
external to him. A similar will to control is suggested by the reiteration
of particular words or phrases in the descriptive passages, a style which
is in some respects reminiscent of Homer's.[16] Countless episodes in the
novel, for instance, close with the topos: "Dann ging Witiko wieder
weiter."[17] The use of repeated epithets such as "Tom Johannes der
Fiedler," "David der Zimmerer," "Stephan der Wagenbauer," and
"Christ Severin der Wollweber" (5,1: 246) likewise calls to mind
Homer's reiterated phrases such as "bright-eyed Athene," and appears
thereby to reflect Stifter's faith in the controlledness and controllability
of existence.

A similar faith in reason seems to inform the gradual development of
both the novel's form and its content. This is another attempt to reach
a rational, all-encompassing perspective that can be achieved only
through patience and mature objectivity. The slow but sure progression
towards this ideal is indicated partly by the repetition of unembellished
verbs such as "gehen," "fragen," and "sagen," and partly by the apparent preciseness of the information. Both features are particularly promi-
nent in the narrator's account of a visit to a church[18]:

> Dann gingen Alle in die Kirche . . .
> Dort kniete der König . . .
> Dann betrachteten sie die Kirche.
> Dann gingen sie noch in die Kirche der heiligen Maria Magdalena
> und in die des heiligen Martin . . . und betrachteten die Kirchen.
> Dann besuchte der König die Gräber . . .
> Dann besah er in der Kammer des Fürstenhofes die Bastschuhe
> des Herzoges Přemysl.
> Dann ging er in den großen Saal. (5,2: 114)

The same reverent emphasis on objective precision is maintained
throughout the novel by the consistently formal, even statuesque, mode
of expression found in statements such as "Auf den zweiten Tag nach
diesem Tage"; "Witiko erhob sich von seinem Sitze"; "Da erhob sich

der Bischof von Prag von seinem Stuhle . . . Und der Bischof setzte sich wieder auf seinen Stuhl nieder" (5,2: 35, 53, 285). The same mode of expression is reflected in the way Stifter has the characters answer questions by repeating the words of the questioner. For instance, Witiko's response when asked: "Bist du nach dem Kriege in die Heimath gegangen?" is a measured, litaneutical: "Ich bin in die Heimath gegangen" (5,2: 249). Similarly, when Witiko asks of David: "Hast du Gehilfen . . . ?" the answer is: "Ich habe Gehilfen" (5,2: 261).

Again, however, this style does not express solely the human capacity to gain ultimate access to the universe by means of his reason. It signifies to an equal degree an apparent faith in morality and in man's ability to control his deep passions. In *Witiko*, the scope of this conviction is extended from individual characters to encompass the whole of history. That Stifter viewed the historical novel as a means to satisfy his creative impulses and, simultaneously, his desire to transcend the strife of the individual's passion is made clear in a letter to Heckenast of 8 June 1861:

> Es erscheint mir . . . in historischen Romanen die Geschichte die Hauptsache und die einzelnen Menschen die Nebensache, sie werden von dem großen Strome getragen, und helfen den Strom bilden. Darum steht mir das Epos viel höher als das Drama, und der sogenannte historische Roman erscheint mir als das Epos in ungebundener Rede. (*Briefe*, 339)

The objectivity that this letter extols remains apparently intact throughout the novel. Even the tiniest hint of subjectivity is drowned by the sheer volume of the words that intimate in an almost sacral manner processes in which the individual plays little or no part. Similarly, any conflict in which man's passions could gain the upper hand is avoided. Witiko, for example, is obliged by custom to wait a certain length of time before asking for Bertha's hand in marriage, but any possible tension is dissolved by her telling him in advance that she will accept his future proposal. Likewise, the style of the dialogue strives towards absolute impersonality. We find a litany that attempts to express in a single voice the unity of a whole population, a tendency that is most pronounced in passages such as those which concern formal decisions:

> "Ich rede für größere Sicherheit,"antwortete Diepold.
> "Ich für morgige Entscheidung," sagte Heinrich.
> "Und ihr dort weiterhin?" fragte der Herzog.
> "Für morgige Entscheidung," rief Zwest.
> "Für morgige Entscheidung," rief Jurik der Sohn Juriks.
> "Für morgige Entscheidung," rief Beneda. (5,1: 308)

This style intensifies as the novel gathers momentum and, again, it suggests absolute agreement and fidelity in the population. Witiko's men agree to join Rowno until their leader returns:

> Rowno antwortete: " . . . Wenn ihr euch, bis er wieder da ist, unter meine Leute einordnen wollt, so werden wir zusammen halten, und uns gegenseitig helfen, wenn die Feinde vor die Stadt kommen."
> "Ja, bis er da ist," rief der Schmied.
> "Bis er da ist," rief Philipp.
> "Bis er da ist," riefen mehrere Stimmen. (5,2: 48)

They swear an oath of loyalty to Witiko in the same escalatory manner:

> "Wir gehören nun wieder zu dir, Witiko," rief David der Zimmerer mit heller Stimme.
> "Zu dir," rief Philipp.
> "Zu dir," riefen mehrere Stimmen.
> "Zu dir," riefen dann Alle. (5,2: 108)

Their fealty to Wratislaw is conveyed in the same way:

> Darauf sagte Wladislaw: " . . . Otto, sprich."
> Otto sagte: "Ich rede wie Wratislaw geredet hat."
> Dann sagte Wladislaw: "Leopold, sprich."
> Leopold antwortete: "Ich rede wie Wratislaw."
> Dann sagte Wladislaw: "Spitihněw, sprich."
> Spitihněw entgegnete: "Ich rede genau so wie Wratislaw."
> Dann sagte Wladislaw: "Wladislaw, Sohn Soběslaws, sprich."
> (5,3: 145)[19]

Even when the dialogue is restricted to two individuals, the same unceasing objectivity is apparently sustained. Every conversation, for example, closes in almost the same manner as a prayer, with formulaic words of dismissal:

> "und so gehabe dich wohl."
> "Gehabt euch wohl." (5,3: 75)[20]

Beyond the objectivity of self-control, however, Witiko displays a transcendent idealism in both form and content similar to the idealism embodied in Risach's marble statue. Lunding is one of the critics who recognises this when he writes that the style expresses "das Ewige und Gesetzmäßige,"[21] and Höllerer would appear to agree with him, to judge by his conviction that Stifter's language reflects "jene Ordnung . . . , die, seiner Einsicht nach, in den Dingen und in dem Inneren der Menschen sich zugleich vernehmen läßt."[22] Through its monumental composition, the novel seeks even more insistently than, for example, Der Nachsommer to intimate that the universe is a coherent

whole, regardless of whether its essence be offered or denied to man. This is clearly indicated by both the form and the content of a conversation held between the Cardinal and Witiko:

> "Hocherhabener kirchlicher Fürst," sagte Witiko, "ich suchte zu thun, wie es die Dinge fordern, und wie die Gewohnheit will, die mir in der Kindheit eingepflanzt worden ist."
> "Und der Glaube, mein Sohn, den der gute Priester Benno in dein Herz gesenkt hat," sagte der Kardinal . . . "Und wenn du zu thun strebst, was die Dinge fordern, so wäre gut, wenn alle wüßten, was die Dinge fordern, und wenn alle thäten, was die Dinge fordern; denn dann thäten sie den Willen Gottes."
> "Oft weiß ich nicht, was die Dinge fordern," sprach Witiko.
> "Dann folge dem Gewissen, und du folgst den Dingen," sagte der Kardinal. (5,3: 173–4)

There is a kind of gravity attributed to each of the German words that probably could not be rendered in English; a weight by means of which Stifter attempts to connote the divine essence of these unspecified "things" that make up the universe. We find the same process at work in the "ontic" mode that, as we have already seen, dominates works such as "Der fromme Spruch" and *Der Nachsommer*. In *Witiko* we read, for example:

> Es waren schöne [Pferde] da . . . In engeren Ständen waren die Kühe der Stier und die Kälber. Dann waren unter flachen Gewölben die Ställe für die Schweine . . . in einem eigenen Gehege dieser Räume waren die Ziegen . . . Für die Gänse und Enten war ein Anger mit einem Teiche. (5,1: 218)

Matz is right to comment on the extremeness of this style, although it is interesting to note that he is not entirely complimentary:

> Mit diesen stilistischen Mitteln führte Stifter eine Tendenz, die auch früher schon in seinen Werken angelegt war, zum Extrem: die Tendenz zum objektivierenden, gleichsam ontologischen Schreiben, zu einer Epik, die den Menschen der Gewalt des Tatsächlichen unterordnet. Die Welt ist, wie sie ist — so könnte man den metaphysischen Grundton benennen, auf den der *Witiko* gestimmt ist. Ein Autor, der sich auf ein solches Erzählen einläßt, hat offenkundig weder vor der Wiederholung noch vor der puren Tautologie Angst.[23]

When confronted with a thousand pages in which there is practically no variation in this style, many people may well find themselves forced to agree with Hebbel's sneering criticism of *Der Nachsommer* (and, by implication, of the whole of Stifter's later work): "Ein Inventar ist ebenso interessant,"[24] or with the reviewer who wrote simply: "Diese Er-

zählung [*Witiko*] ist, soweit sie in dem ersten Bande vorliegt, im höchsten Grade langweilig."[25] However, as we have already seen, the monotony that characterises Stifter's later works is far from dull. We should perhaps again take our cue not from Hebbel but from the more sharp-eyed Thomas Mann, whose admiration of *Witiko* stems from its very monotony:

> Auch ich habe den *Witiko* lange gemieden, weil ich ihn für langweilig hielt. Und dabei wußte ich doch, daß es höchst abenteuerliche Arten des Langweiligen gibt und daß der Langweiligkeit nur ein wenig Genie beigemischt zu sein braucht, um in eine Sphäre zu versetzen [*sic*], worin von langer und kurzer Weile all-überall nicht mehr die Rede sein kann. *Witiko* ist ein solches Traum-Abenteuer einer Langweiligkeit höchster Art.[26]

Once our ear has become attuned to the curiously obsessive tenor of Stifter's style, it seems hardly credible that *Witiko* could have been so rapidly dismissed, or that the hapless Margaret Gump could believe that "this factual style, which often verges on the dry, affects readers in different ways. Some will find it boring, whereas others will find that it conveys great peace and quiet."[27] Even in passages that, so one presumes, are partly intended to uphold pious gradualness in both form and content, it is impossible to miss the "manic obsession" that Adorno recognises in the aesthetic, the "Neigung zum Exzessiven, Elementar-Katastrophalen, Pathologischen" of which Thomas Mann speaks. The precarious stylistic tightrope that Stifter walks in *Witiko* between moderation and mania becomes perceptible, for example, in a repetitive passage that depicts a religious ritual:

> Als der Gottesdienst beendet war, sprach der Pfarrer der Kriegesgemeinde die Danksworte an Gott den Allmächtigen für Errettung aus den Gefahren und Abwendung des Unheils vor, und die Krieger sprachen die Worte nach. Und alle Menschen, welche vor den Schranken knieten, sprachen die Worte nach. Dann sprach der Pfarrer die Gebetworte für die Verstorbenen vor, und die Krieger sprachen sie nach. Und die Menschen vor den Schranken sprachen sie nach. (5,3: 77)

Within the affirmatory grandiloquence of its style is a heart-rending sense of fragility and imminent collapse (in this way, the effect of *Witiko* is similar only to that of a Bruckner symphony). The "moral" dimension of the novel is by no means as unshakeable as it may initially appear. The manner of expression employed by Stifter does indeed on one level imply the security of reasonable tranquillity — but the tension of the work lies to no small extent in the way in which the same mode so poignantly expresses doubt and fear. And the more we immerse our-

selves in the novel's flood of words, the more inescapable becomes the sense of menace lurking within the idyllic perfection. An ominous ground bass constantly counterpoints the serene descant of the style:

> Das Bett mit der Bärendecke steht noch in dem Gemache, und der Schrein steht an dem Bette, und in dem Schreine ist das rothe Beutelchen mit dem goldenen Kreuzlein. (5,3: 214)

Or:

> Es glänzte Wasser im Monde, es glänzte das Gras um das Wasser, und die Büsche daran glänzten auch, aus ihnen ragten dunkle Giebel wie Dächer von Hütten empor, und oben war der Mond in gelblichen Wolken. (5,1: 185)[28]

In a sense, these extracts could be seen as even more idyllic re-writes of the passages in "Turmalin" and "Kazensilber" that I singled out for attention earlier. Again, we find diminutives and verbs that imply intact perfection, but it is again an excessive impeccability suggested by this manner of writing that makes the whole idyllic mode come across as threatening.

The menace or *Unmaß* in the work, then, is not something which somehow manages to show itself *despite* the repetition with its seeming aura of security: the tension threatening the idyll lies *within* this iterative style. In this respect, it is interesting to consider *Witiko* as a kind of monumental fairy tale. More distinctly than in any other of Stifter's works, we find in this novel rhythms and repetitions that echo those of fairy tales, and so convey a sense of blissful beauty and innocence. For example, threefold repetition characterises the words attributed to the characters at almost every formal meeting, and this by itself lends the work the charmed air of a fairy tale. Thus we find utterances such as "Das Reich, das Reich, das Reich," "Immer, immer, immer," "deutlich, deutlich, deutlich," "Witiko, Witiko, Witiko," and "Nach Mailand, nach Mailand, nach Mailand," to list but a few (5,2: 79, 321; 5,3: 263, 275, 278).[29] Yet, as in fairy tales, the tension increases as the stylistic repetition escalates: in this case, the constantly chiming words become like a mocking, ironic chorus, not least because of what they actually say. There is nothing sweetly reassuring about "Verrath, Verrath, Verrath!" (5,2: 92), "Die Strafe, die Strafe, die Strafe" (5,3: 263); "Ans Kreuz, ans Kreuz, ans Kreuz" (5,3: 267, 268). The underlying threat of this work is subtly but powerfully displayed in the iterative conversation which takes place when Witiko and Bertha first chance upon one another in the forest:

> "Ach, was ihr für schöne Haare habt!" sagte das Mädchen.
> "Und was du für rothe Wangen hast," erwiederte er.

"Und wie blau eure Augen sind," sagte sie.
"Und wie braun und groß die deinen," antwortete er.
"Und wie ihr freundlich sprecht," sagte sie.
"Und wie du lieblich bist," antwortete er. (5,1: 35)

This is surely one of the most typically fairy-tale-like passages of the whole novel, if not in Stifter's entire oeuvre. We are given the iconically perfect details of the rosy cheeks, the blue eyes, the flowing hair, and the beautiful, nameless "Mädchen." In its mesmeric rhythm, too, this exchange bears a striking resemblance to those found in fairy tales; in this case, it is unmistakably reminiscent of the climactic dialogue in *Rotkäppchen* (Little Red Riding Hood):

> "Ei, Großmutter, was hast du für große Ohren!" "Daß ich dich besser hören kann." "Ei, Großmutter, was hast du für große Augen!" "Daß ich dich besser sehen kann." "Ei, Großmutter, was hast du für große Hände!" "Daß ich dich besser packen kann." "Aber, Großmutter, was hast du für ein entsetzlich großes Maul!" "Daß ich dich besser fressen kann." Kaum hatte der Wolf das gesagt, so tat er einen Satz aus dem Bette und verschlang das arme Rotkäppchen.[30]

Yet how implicitly threatening this parallelism makes the *Witiko* passage appear! The stylistically analogous scene in the fairy tale is that in which the young girl is devoured by the wolf — and wolves are one of the most potent images in Stifter's earlier work for man's rampant sexual potential.[31] Can we not, then, infer from this stylistic similarity that a wolf subliminally lurks in the enchanting encounter in *Witiko*? And could not Witiko himself be viewed as an excessively idyllic remake of the Major in "Brigitta," the character whose latent wolfishness is most clearly suggested? If it seems implausible to cast such doubts on the fairy tale paradise that Stifter appears to offer us, one should also take into account the iconic depiction of the protagonist which immediately precedes his conversation with Bertha:

> Bei diesen Worten nahm er die Lederhaube sammt ihrem Anhange von seinem Haupte, und eine Fülle schöner blonder Haare rollte auf seinen Nacken herab. Die Haube legte er in das Gras. (5,1: 35)

The very picture of boyishly innocent beauty? It may be so. But it bears a discomfiting similarity to the passage in "Der Hochwald," written over twenty years earlier, where the child-seducer Ronald stands suddenly revealed before the walls of the beleaguered castle (thereby provoking an orgy of slaughter and devastation):

> der Helm entfiel ihm — ein ganzer Wall von blonden Locken rollte in diesem Augenblicke über seinen Nacken — — . . . (1,4: 314)

This adds a much more sinister dimension to the character of Witiko, suggesting that beneath his golden loveliness there simmers the same glowing passion that destroys everything touched by Ronald in "Der Hochwald." (And, no less disturbingly, it also works the other way round: Ronald becomes Witiko-like.) By extension, the conversation between Witiko and Bertha is a heavily idealised and ritualised — and thus excessively *controlled* — re-write of the explosively *uncontrolled* declarations at the climax of "Der Hochwald." There is the burning excess of Ronald's feelings on the one hand ("siehe, tropfenweise will ich dieses Blut für dich vergießen . . . — — nimm mir mein Leben, nimm mir die Seele aus dem Leibe, damit du nur siehest, wie ich dich liebe," 1,4: 289) and, on the other, the almost unbearable intensity of the passage in which Clarissa's resolve to renounce the man who made love to her when she was still but a child suddenly melts away:

> o Ronald, ich liebe dich ja, ich kann mir nicht helfen, und hättest du tausend Fehler, ich liebte dich doch — ich lieb' dich unermeßlich, mehr als Vater und Geschwister, mehr als mich selbst und Alles, mehr als ich es begreifen kann . . . (1,4: 289)

In *Witiko* there is no outpouring of emotion, no mention of any passion that is even moderate in nature, let alone "unermeßlich," and yet the incessant, manic control suggests latent *Unmaß* just as emphatically and disturbingly as does "Der Hochwald." The manner in which the lovers in *Witiko* protest complete purity works for the reader in much the same way:

> "Du hast an dem schönen großen Steine neben dem Waldsaume vor zwei Jahren zu mir gesagt, Bertha,' antwortete Witiko: 'baue dir ein Haus, Witiko, und wenn dann noch keine Makel an dir ist, so folge ich dir, und harre bei dir bis zum Tode. Nun baue ich mir ein Haus, und bin gekommen, dich zu fragen, ob eine Makel an mir ist?"
> "Es ist keine Makel an dir, Witiko," antwortete Bertha.
> "So wirst du mir in das Haus folgen?" fragte Witiko.
> "Ich werde dir in das Haus folgen," entgegnete Bertha.
> "Und wirst dort harren bis zu dem Tode?" fragte Witiko.
> "Ich werde harren bis zu dem Tode," antwortete Bertha.
> "So ist gesprochen, was zuerst gesprochen werden sollte," sagte Witiko. "Bertha, Bertha, sei mir tausendmal gegrüßt."
> "Sei tausend und tausend Mal gegrüßt, Witiko," antwortete Bertha.
> Und sie reichten sich die Hände, hielten sich an denselben, und schauten sich in das Angesicht. (5,3: 121)

The intense focus on the words "keine Makel" invokes the very opposite.[32] The untouchedness suggested by the scene is too studied, too

perfect; the rhythm of their conversation is not the "moral" rhythm of the *Bunte Steine* preface, but the tense, relentless tolling of the bell which marks the frailty of their immaculate paradise.

The Apollonian idyll is thus subtly under constant threat of contamination by the forces associated with human sexuality. Nevertheless, sensual chaos is only one aspect of the human drama that reveals itself through Stifter's increasingly manic tendency towards concealment. In his drive towards objectivity, he strips away all the features of his writing that could explicitly denote *any* kind of emotion. This, of course, is not restricted to his treatment of *Witiko*, but reflects an obsession manifest in all the later work. It is clearly evident in the *Letzte Mappe*, for example, the other story that occupied Stifter's creative mind whilst he was writing *Witiko*. This differs from both the book and journal versions of "Die Mappe" in its ritenuto style — and yet it is this very style that articulates to a far greater degree the constant tension within apparently tranquil self-control, and the fragility of the faith in heavenly comfort. The changes that Stifter makes to the passage in which the "gentle" old colonel ("sanftmüthiger Obrist") recounts his feelings after the death of his wife are in this respect revealing. The full impact of the final version's account can be appreciated only when it is seen in the context of its two predecessors, hence all three passages deserve to be quoted *in extenso*. The passionate response of the colonel is made very evident in the journal version:

> Ihr heißt mich einen guten Mann; mag seyn, daß ich es bin — *das* habe ich mir zugeschworen, als ich grollend brütete und grübelte, wozu denn nun der Herr des Himmels gerade das, gerade das gethan, gerade das — — aber als er keine Antwort gab, und liebreich seine Sonne, seine Sterne, seinen Regen und Thau, seine goldenen Früchte alle heraufführte, da erkannte ich, wie mein Unglück in diesem unermeßlichen Haushalte eigentlich ein unbedeutend Ding sey, ein Verlust, wie der einer kleinen goldnen Mücke — ja nicht einmal ein Verlust, so wie das Senfkorn, das in lockeres Erdreich fällt, vergeht, aber nicht verloren ist — — ... Gott brauchte einen Engel im Himmel, und einen guten Menschen auf Erden, deßhalb mußte sie sterben. (1,2: 37–8; Stifter's emphasis)

The more controlled mode employed by the Stifter of the book version suggests an increase in the man's self-control:

> — Dann schien die Sonne, wie alle Tage, es wuchs das Getreide, das sie im Herbste angebaut hatten, die Bäche rannen durch die Thäler hinaus — — nur daß sie allein dahin war, wie der Verlust einer goldenen Mücke. — Und wie ich in jener Zeit mit Gott haderte, hatte ich gar nichts, als daß ich mir fest dachte, ich wolle so gut werden, wie

sie, und wolle thun, wie sie thäte, wenn sie noch lebte. Seht, Doctor, ich habe mir damals eingebildet, Gott brauche einen Engel im Himmel und einen guten Menschen auf Erden: deßhalb mußte sie sterben. — (1,5: 62)

In the *Letzte Mappe*, however, we read:

Und der Tag verging, und der nächste verging, und immer mehrere vergingen, und die Sonne stand am Himmel, die Getreide wuchsen, die Bäche rauschten, nur daß sie dahin war, und daß es war wie der Verlust einer goldenen Mücke. Und wie ich in jener Zeit fast mit Gott haderte, hatte ich nichts, gar nichts, als daß ich mir fest dachte, ich wolle so gut werden wie sie, und wolle tun, wie sie täte, wenn sie noch lebte. Seht, Doktor, ich habe mir damals eingebildet, Gott brauche einen Engel im Himmel und einen guten Menschen auf Erden, deshalb mußte sie sterben. (*MSB* 180)

In this version, his anguish might appear to be toned down. The darkly menacing verbs "brüten" and "grübeln" are replaced by the simple "haben," "sein," and "gehen" in the *Letzte Mappe*; the aposiopesis that suggests his pain in both the earlier versions is rejected in favour of the flowing syntactical continuity of the final version; the rhythmic monotone of the repetend "und" appears to measure the even flow of time, the gentle continuity of nature of which the apparently philosophical old man speaks. As Hermann Kunisch would have it, the *Letzte Mappe* passage illustrates "das Selbstverständliche der Natur, ihr gleichmäßiger, unbeirrter Gang, ihr Geduld und Vertrauen aussagendes Wesen."[33] But this is surely one of the most poignant and poetic evocations of grief that Stifter ever wrote.[34] With its combination of brutal economy and rhythmic pulse the passage no longer merely "describes" but vividly *actualises* the terrible gulf between the agony of individuals and the serenity-cum-indifference of the All. The sombre repetition of "und" serves superbly to express the omnipresence of loss, the sense of abiding and absolute bereftness. That this is a condition rather than a transient feeling is made graphically clear by the one laconic sentence that follows shortly after this passage in the *Letzte Mappe* (and which has no analogue in the earlier versions): "Mein Schmerz dauerte aber immer fort und immer fort" (*MSB* 180). The man's grief is not just the eruptive emotion of the journal version which surges forth and then dies down; it is an enduring black emptiness:

A grief without a pang, void, dark, and drear,
A stifled, drowsy, unimpassioned grief,
Which finds no natural outlet, no relief,
In word, or sigh, or tear —[35]

This bleak despair is compounded by the lack of divine consolation offered by the paragraph. It initially appears that God is challenged to a greater degree in the journal version, with the threefold repetition of "gerade das," but this feeling is again like a firework which dangerously flares up but just as quickly turns to harmless ashes in the face of God's all-embracing love. The *Letzte Mappe* is less explicit in its questioning, but the natural and celestial indifference to human suffering with which it presents us is quite stunning. Like the old colonel in the narrative, the critic Matz tries to wrest some kind of ultimate sense from these events — but it is wholly unconvincing when all he can offer is: "Das offenkundig Sinnlose *muß* einen Sinn haben."[36] Significantly, the *Letzte Mappe* employs a suppositional subjunctive in the colonel's attribution of a "meaning" to his wife's sudden death ("Gott *brauche* einen Engel"), whereas is it stated as an indisputable fact in the journal version ("Gott *brauchte* einen Engel"). Furthermore, the rhythm of the passage in the *Letzte Mappe* does not measure the "changing of the seasons"[37]; it stylistically articulates in the most intensely controlled manner a litany in which God has ceased to exist. This mode, which shows Stifter writing at the height of his artistic powers, registers the instability of both reason and divine providence; the fear that beneath these precarious structures there may indeed be "nichts, *gar* nichts."

Notes

[1] See also Helena Ragg-Kirkby, "*Witiko and the Absurd*," in *The Biedermeier and Beyond. Selected Papers from the Symposium held at St. Peter's College, Oxford from 19–21 September 1997*, ed. Roe and Warren (Bern etc.: Lang, 1999), 169–81.

[2] Fritz Novotny perceives a similar development in Stifter's paintings (see *Adalbert Stifter als Maler* [Vienna: Schroll, 1941], 40).

[3] Matz, *Adalbert Stifter*, 371. It is interesting to note that the novel provoked a largely negative reaction among Stifter's contemporaries (see Enzinger, *Stifter im Urteil seiner Zeit*, 264–7).

[4] Lunding, *Adalbert Stifter*, 88.

[5] "In der deutschen Literatur stellt Stifters *Witiko* ein ebenso einmaliges Phänomen dar wie Büchners *Woyzeck*" (Heinz Otto Burger, "Der Stilwille der Unzeitgemäßen in Dichtung und Bildkunst des 19. Jahrhunderts," *Germanisch-Romanische Monatsschrift*, 1 [1950–51]: 295).

[6] Klatt, "Stifter und das Dämonische," 290.

[7] Hermann Hesse, *Gesammelte Werke* (Frankfurt am Main: Suhrkamp, 1976), *Schriften zur Literatur II* (= Band 12), 282.

[8] Thomas Mann, *Miszellen* (Frankfurt am Main and Hamburg: Fischer, 1968), 186.

[9] Hesse, *Gesammelte Werke*, Band 12, 282.

[10] Stern, *Idylls*, 111. Matz also refers to what he calls the novel's "aura of unreadableness" and the "monotony of the narrative tone" (*Adalbert Stifter*, 366).

[11] Hesse, *Gesammelte Werke*, Band 12, 282.

[12] Hesse, *Gesammelte Werke*, Band 12, 281.

[13] Barnes, "The Function of Conversations and Speeches in *Witiko*," 24.

[14] See Franz Hüller, *Adalbert Stifters "Witiko"* (Nuremberg: Hans Carl, 1954), 55.

[15] This is elaborated upon later by Benno, who claims that atrocities will only cease when the requisite ordering principle has been established: "So ist es oft gewesen, und so wird es wieder sein, wenn nicht ein fester Brauch errichtet wird, wie der Herzog nach dem Tode des frühern Herzoges folgen soll, und wenn nicht der heilige Glaube tief gegründet, und in schönen Ordnungen durch das ganze Land geleitet wird, daß er die Herzen erleuchtet" (5,3: 92).

[16] Stifter's admiration of the *Iliad's* historical form is made explicit in a letter to Heckenast of 8 June 1861 (see *Briefe*, 339).

[17] Variations on this theme are repeated numerous times; see, for example, 5,1: 198; 5,2: 137, 160, 169, 209; 5,3: 11, 176, 179, 283.

[18] One of the many interesting features of Witiko is that it gives the impression of a first person narrative, although it is actually written in the third person. We hear and see things only as Witiko hears and sees them. For example, we are not told that "der Mann in dem braunen Gewande" (5,2: 141 and *passim*) is Zdik until Witiko himself realises this. Similarly, no omniscient narrator tells us which characters are actually present in many of the scenes: those whom Witiko himself recognises are listed and the others are simply "mehrere, welche Witiko nicht kannte" (5,1: 237) or "Männer und Herren . . . , welche Witiko nicht kannte" (5,1: 272).

[19] This mode of writing characterises almost every decision in the novel. The decision to advance into battle is conveyed in this way: "'Ihr seid Tröpfe, und also, lieben Brüder, vorwärts,' rief Wratislaw. 'Vorwärts,' rief Wladislaw, der Sohn Soběslaws. 'Wir müssen nach vorwärts,' rief Bogdan. 'Vorwärts, vorwärts,' riefen mehrere" (5,2: 87). Even praise is given by the duke in an obsessively repetitive way: "'Lob und Dank euch Allen. Lob und Dank denen, die Lob und Dank nicht mehr hören können, weil sie den Tod herrlicher Krieger gefunden haben; Lob und Dank denen, welche Wunden an ihrem

Körper tragen . . . ; Lob und Dank auch dem edlen Herzoge Sobeslaw . . . ; Lob und Dank allen Vorgängern . . . ; Lob und Dank denen, welche aus dem ganzen Lande sich zu mir gesellt . . . haben . . . ; und Lob und Dank denen, die dem Feinde den Muth genommen haben: das größte Lob und den größten Dank aber dem, ohne den Alles vergeblich gewesen wäre, dem großen dem gerechten dem allmächtigen Gott . . . Und nun noch einmal: Gruß und Dank . . . , und zum dritten Male: Gruß und Dank.' 'Gruß und Dank,' riefen alle Männer einstimmig, und schlugen an ihre Schwerter" (5,2: 102–3).

[20] For variations on this theme see, for example, 5,1: 29, 105, 211; 5,2: 140, 234, 244, 254, 286, 306; 5,3: 42, 56, 62, 75, 84, 94, 139, 175, 189, 205, 299, 300.

[21] Lunding, *Adalbert Stifter*, 106.

[22] Höllerer, "Stifter," 377.

[23] Matz, *Adalbert Stifter*, 367–8.

[24] Hebbel, *Werke*, vol. 3, 683.

[25] Cited in Enzinger, *Stifter im Urteil seiner Zeit*, 267.

[26] Mann, *Miszellen*, 186–7.

[27] Gump, *Adalbert Stifter*, 130.

[28] A similar passage is found in 5,2: 169: "Es öffnete sich . . . ein kleines Thürchen in dem Thore, und unter dem Thürchen stand ein Mann, der eine veilchenfarbene Haube und ein veilchenfarbenes Mäntelchen hatte."

[29] The constant use of threefold repetition is one of the most ominous aspects of Stifter's style in *Witiko*, not least because it escalates as the novel progresses. See, for example, 5,2: 108, 279, 295, 309; 5,3: 36, 58, 158, 184, 196, 258–9, 259, 278.

[30] Jacob and Wilhelm Grimm, *Kinder- und Hausmärchen gesammelt durch die Brüder Grimm* (Munich: Winkler, 1990), 178. It is also worth noting that Little Red Riding Hood encounters the wolf in the forest, as Bertha does Witiko (and Clarissa does Ronald).

[31] This is particularly evident in "Brigitta." Here, the heroine's boundary wall does indeed protect her gentle deer from an external threat, namely the wasteland's minacious wolves. The narrator and the Major both encourage us to believe that she has been entirely successful in keeping the wild marauders safely outside her terrain: "[man] ging . . . Schritt für Schritt durch jede Stelle des Parkes, um zu sehen, ob man nicht etwa einen Wolf zu künftiger Brut mit eingemauert habe. Aber es war keiner zugegen" (1,5: 463–4). These assertions seem to be confirmed as the attack on Gustav takes place in the wasteland, outside her wall (1,5: 468). Yet a closer reading suggests that the wolves are altogether symbolic rather than naturalistic; that they represent the passion and turbulence latent within the Major. As the latter dashes to rescue

Gustav, the narrator is shocked to see that he is "fast selber wie ein Raubthier" (1,5: 468), and this is a most explicit clue encouraging us to see the wolves as a symbolic expression of the *human* predator's dormant destructiveness. It is he who possesses the rapacious potential of a "Raubthier": he preys on the "gazelle" Gabriele, wreaking inestimable damage once he finally has her in his arms. Both naturalistically and symbolically, the lupine potential has been kept under control for many years, and at the symbolic level it remains under control. What happens "naturalistically" is a reminder of what *can* happen if the inner wolf is given any scope. See also Irmscher, *Wirklichkeitserfahrung und gegenständliche Darstellung*, 61, and Reddick, "Wild Beyond," 122–3.

[32] This focus on immaculacy is emphasised further by Witiko's declaration to Heinrich von Schauenberg: "Eure hochedle Tochter Bertha . . . hat zu mir bei dem großen Steine an dem Waldessaume gesagt: Baue dir ein Haus, Witiko, und wenn dann noch keine Makel an dir ist, so folge ich dir, und harre bei dir bis zum Tode. Gestattet, hoher Herr und hocherhabene Frau, daß ich Bertha sage, ich baue mir nun ein Haus, und daß ich sie frage, ob eine Makel an mir ist" (5,3: 120). Earlier in the novel, even the immaculacy of the floor is stressed: "der Fußboden war gewaschen, und der Buchentisch war so gescheuert, daß keine Makel an ihm war" (5,2: 288).

[33] Hermann Kunisch, "Die Ordnung des Seins bei Adalbert Stifter," in Hermann Kunisch, *Kleine Schriften* (Berlin and Munich: Duncker und Humblot, 1968), 360–1.

[34] Even the more astute critics who write about the story fail to recognise the astounding devastation implied in these lines (many of them do not even mention this episode). Paul Böckmann, for example, claims of this passage: "Die Fremdheit des Geschehenen bleibt das zentrale Thema, wenn auch die subjektive Klage zurückgedrängt wird und statt dessen das Gleichmaß der Verrichtungen, der Wechsel der Tage und ihrer Forderungen stärker zur Geltung kommen, wie sie schon das Dasein der Verstorbenen bestimmten. Der 'Zweck der Allheit' bleibt verborgen, aber er wirkt im Gleichmaß des Daseins" ("Die epische Objektivität in Stifters Erzählung Die Mappe meines Urgroßvaters," in *Stoffe Formen Strukturen: Studien zur deutschen Literatur. Hans Heinrich Borcherdt zum 75. Geburtstag*, ed. Fuchs and Motekat [Munich: M. Hueber, 1962], 407).

[35] Samuel Taylor Coleridge, "Dejection: An Ode," in Samuel Taylor Coleridge, *Poems*, ed. John Beer (London: Dent, 1986), 280.

[36] Matz, *Adalbert Stifter*, 169; his emphasis.

[37] Gump relates the rhythm of Stifter's prose to nature in this way, particularly in the context of *Witiko*: "there is a rhythmic, orderly pattern in *Witiko*, as there is in nature with its constant change of seasons" (*Adalbert Stifter*, 129).

6: *Witiko* and the Ineffable

"so außerordentlich, wie es gar nicht auszusprechen ist"
(*Witiko*)

IN THIS PERSPECTIVE, the style of *Witiko* registers the fragility of the positive tableau Stifter purports to paint of security and unambiguous meaning, and it opens out a vision of the abyss. This is most effectively summed up by Peter Rosei:

> Nur schwer kann man sich bei näherem Studium der Stifter'schen Dichtungen dem Gefühl entziehen, daß unter den so treuherzig und ideal geschilderten Verhältnissen der Abgrund offen ist, daß Stifter verzweifelt versucht, ihn zu überbrücken oder, noch besser, überhaupt zu verbergen. Je perfekter ihm dieses Vorhaben gelingt, desto unabweisbarer wird die Ahnung von der Tiefe.[1]

If we follow this line of argument, we no longer find merely a modicum of tension pervading the edifice of perfect repetition that Stifter builds over the abyss. I suggested in the introduction that an alternative sub-text can be descried by the reader who is alive to the chasms lurking beneath the gleaming surfaces of the earlier texts. This is true even in parts of the *Letzte Mappe*, where there is quite literally a chasm: the abyss into which the wife of the colonel plunges to her death. The surface of *Witiko*, though, displays no such chasms, nor even any hairline cracks: Stifter has abandoned the *Inselspitzen* technique alluded to in "Der Hochwald" (1,4: 219). But repetition on an unprecedented scale is no longer just a means of expressing a tension between text and sub-text: the *excess* of order and the *excess* of repetition are themselves the carriers of a magnificently dystopian vision. Moreover, any distinction one might want to make between medium and message is simply irrelevant in the case of *Witiko*, for its action, even more so than in "Der fromme Spruch," is so minimal that it merits little consideration. Yet I believe that this is one of the most gripping pieces of writing Stifter ever produced, because a vision of otherness is conveyed wholly through his unique use of language and style. The novel can perhaps only be fully appreciated if it is approached in almost the same manner as a piece of music. Like music, it is held together solely by its mesmeric rhythm and repetition; more specifically, its effect can be compared to that of the minimalist compositions that it in a sense prefigures. Thus we no longer

find the isolated passages of disturbingly grave simplicity displayed by stories such as "Turmalin" and "Kazensilber": the whole composition is based on a relentless deluge of rhythmic monotony. The specific sonority of the work is established from the moment the story line is inaugurated in the second paragraph, and painstakingly sustained thereafter throughout the course of some one thousand pages:

> Zur Zeit, da in Deutschland der dritte Conrad, der erste aus dem Geschlechte der Hohenstaufen, herrschte, da Baiern der stolze Heinrich inne hatte, da Leopold der Freigebige Markgraf in Österreich war, da Sobeslaw der Erste auf dem Herzogstuhle der Böhmen saß, und da man das Jahr des Heiles 1138 schrieb: ritt in der Schlucht zwischen dem Berge des Oberhauses und dem des Nonngütleins . . . ein Mann von der Donau gegen das mitternächtige Hügelland hinaus. (5,1: 15–16)

Yet this monotone is far from being tedious, as Thomas Mann recognised:

> Es ist doch mehr und anderes als das bekannte noble ennui. Es ist ein stiller, blasser, pedantischer Zauber, der fester hält, als das meiste Interessante und einem demonstriert, was [sic], welches Maß von Langweiligkeit unter Umständen möglich ist, möglich gemacht werden kann.[2]

Again, it is the endless repetition that comes across as obsessive; it is not that dimensions of mania allow themselves to be glimpsed through cracks in the surface. On the contrary, the more perfectly moderated the surface seems to become, the more manic and immoderate its effect. The unceasing assertion of measure, order, and control sets up an inherent paradox: the assertion itself becomes immoderate, chaotic, uncontrolled. Although the unrelenting use of this mode makes it difficult to single out any one textual example of the style of *Witiko* for particular consideration, it is nonetheless worth noting that the novel does not exist in some sphere completely independent of Stifter's previous works: what it *does* do is take small, isolated elements of these earlier works and expand them in such a way that what is initially threatening becomes utterly terrifying. In "Der beschriebene Tännling" (The Inscribed Little Fir-tree, 1850), for instance, the repetition of the word "ging" (which, in turn, is not in the journal version of the story) unsettles the reader:

> Hanns ging von seinem Walde nach Pichlern.
> Als er dort angekommen war, ging er zu dem weißen Häuslein; aber er fand es verschlossen . . .
> Er ging zu seiner Schwester und zog die Sonntagskleider an.

> Dann ging er wieder zu dem Häuschen, das noch verschlossen
> war . . .
> Hanns ging nun in die grauen Steine. Er sezte sich dort auf einen
> derselben nieder, und hielt den Kopf fest in beiden Händen, gleich-
> sam als warte er. (1,6: 420)[3]

The "sameness" of the language is perhaps on one level an attempt to
re-create the reassuring sameness of everyday life. But the same does
not spell out sameness: it spells out *excess*; and *Witiko* goes further still.
As in "Der beschriebene Tännling," the rhythmic minimalism of the
language does not suggest unruffled objectivity. It implies a dimension
of calm but all the more monstrous terror that seems as if it will never
end:

> Witiko ging nun mit den Führern rechts von seinem Gezelte zu dem
> weißen Banner . . . Dann ging er wieder weiter rechts . . . Dann ging
> er zu dem weißen Banner der Männer . . . dann zu dem blauen Ban-
> ner der Männer . . . dann zu dem weißen Kreuze der Männer . . .
> dann zu der Stange, auf welche die Männer vom Eckschlage Geierfed-
> ern gebunden hatten . . . Dann ging er wieder zurück bis zu seinem
> Gezelte, und ging von demselben links zu dem weißen Banner . . .
> und dann weiter links zu dem rosenrothen Banner . . . und dann zu
> dem rothen Kreuze . . . und dann zu dem gelben Fähnlein . . . und
> dann zu der Stange mit dem grünen Kranze . . . und dann zu der
> Stange mit den himmelblauen Bändern . . . Dann ging er zu den Rei-
> tern . . . Dann ging Witiko zu den Männern der Mugrauer Haide . . .
> Dann ging er zu denen vom schwarzen Bache . . . hierauf ging Witiko
> zu den Männern der unteren Moldau . . . Dann ging er zu den Män-
> nern vom Rathschlage . . . Darnach ging er weiter zu denen von Eck-
> schlage . . . er [ging] wieder an allen Leuten zurück . . . Darnach ging
> Witiko zu den Leuten von Friedberg . . . Dann ging er zu denen der
> Steinleithe . . . Dann ging Witiko zu den Männern der Friedau . . .
> Dann ging er zu denen des Kirchenschlages . . . Dann ging Witiko zu
> den Männern der Waldmoldau, des Heurafels und der Stift. (5,3: 11–
> 12)[4]

This is no exception, but one example of an obsessively "minimalist"
narrative that for a thousand pages ritually heaps up verbs with hardly
any variation, "gehen," "kommen," "sprechen," "haben," and "sein"
occurring most frequently, and being featured not for their "meaning"
but for the spell-binding rhythm that they create. A similar stylistic
principle operates in the repetition that marks the novel's dialogue:

> "Und die Herzoge saßen indessen auf ihrem herrschenden Stuh-
> le," sagte Witiko.
> "Ja, die Herzoge, die Herzoge," entgegnete der Scharlachreiter.

Er wendete sich um, und rief: "Der Mann da, der neben mir rei-
tet, frägt um die Herzoge des Landes, meine Freunde."
"Ich meine nur die Herzoge, die zu jener Zeit gewesen sind,"
sagte Witiko.
"Ja, die Herzoge, die Herzoge, nicht wahr, meine Freunde, das ist
so ein Ding, die Herzoge," rief der Scharlachreiter. (5,1: 81–2)

"Nun du Ledermann," sagte der Scharlachreiter hierauf, "du hast von
den Herzogen gesagt, du hast um die Herzoge gefragt, jetzt habe ich
dir Herzoge genug genannt, und habe dir von Herzogen viel erzählt.
Und weil ich dir von Herzogen viel erzählt habe, und weil ich dir von
Geschlechtern viel erzählt habe, und von ihren wilden Sitten, und von
uns und unsern guten Sitten, so könntest du jetzt auch von dir und
deinem Wesen etwas offenbaren, das uns freut." (5,1: 91–2)

This is the mode that conveys most graphically a vision of the abyss.
Wildbolz is one of the few critics to realise that this very manner of expression is itself eloquent, as is made clear when he states of the author:
"Was er inhaltlich-vordergründig nicht zu leisten vermag, erscheint im
Erzählrhythmus."[5] Unfortunately, however, Wildbolz's critical ear is
attuned solely to the earlier works, and he shows himself to be curiously
deaf to the rhythmic power of the later ones: "Von dem, was potentiell
bis zum *Nachsommer* in den besten Texten an Rhythmus und Kraft an-
gelegt ist, bleibt wenig mehr zu verspüren."[6] He is particularly scathing
about *Witiko*: his sole comment on the novel in this context is that its
style becomes a ritual "das sich allzurasch bis zur Monotonie hin auf-
löst."[7] Here, he either denies or fails to perceive the uncanny quality of
the monodic mode of this work, in which the individual elements of the
form gain much of their significance from the total rhythm that they
create. Stifter's style in *Witiko* is its content: here, the rhythm is itself
part of the text's "message." This is suggested by the importance attributed to the rhythm of the conversation between Bertha and her
mother in which mother addresses daughter concerning a meeting pro-
posed by Witiko:

"Willst du ihn hören, und auch mit ihm sprechen?"
"Ich will ihn hören, und mit ihm sprechen." (5,3: 121)

Similarly, the answer to a statement made by Welislaw appears to have
been written with particular consideration for its rhyme and rhythm,
both of which serve to place the novel in a sphere far beyond the
boundaries of conventional nineteenth-century prose style:

"Ich aber rufe," sagte Welislaw, "Leib und Leben und Gut und
Blut für die Ehre und den erlauchten Ritter, den König."

"Leib und Leben und Gut und Blut," riefen die Männer.
                                                    (5,3: 277)

Again, the rhythmic menace of this mode builds up momentum in the
depictions of formal assemblies:

> "Erhabene Sprossen des Stammes Přemysl," sagte nun Wladislaw,
> " . . . Die Männer und Herren, die in meinem Rathe in Prag sind, die
> Männer und Herren, die zu mir nach Prag gekommen sind, die Män-
> ner und Herren, welche die Boten gehört haben, die von mir in das
> ganze Land gesendet worden sind, haben erfahren, daß ich die Worte
> zu dem Herzoge Konrad gesagt habe, und daß ich die Antwort von
> dem Herzoge Konrad erhalten habe . . . ; daß ich die Worte zu dem
> Herzoge Konrad gesagt habe, und daß ich die Antwort von dem Her-
> zoge Konrad erhalten habe . . . ; und ihr alle habet jetzt gehöret, daß
> ich die Worte zu dem Herzoge Konrad gesagt habe, und daß ich die
> Antwort von dem Herzoge Konrad erhalten habe, da wir gesammelt
> auf dem Wege nach Mähren sind." (5,2: 317–18)

This style is quite unlike that of any of Stifter's predecessors or contemporaries. It is absolutely and uncompromisingly beyond the pale. As
such, it may seem that *Witiko* has little in common with other works
such as the earlier *Studien*, with their numerous dual perspectives; the
black, black abysses gaping beneath the beautiful sunny skies. There is
no chasm "ohne Maß und Grenze in die Tiefe gehend" as there is in
"Der Condor" (1,4: 27), no "Unmaß des Schmerzes und der Zärtlich-
keit" as there is in "Der Hochwald" (1,4: 316); there is no "shameful
secret" of sexual or childhood trauma as there is in "Brigitta," "Kalkstein," "Der Hagestolz," "Die Narrenburg" (to name just a few); none
of the terrifying zones of otherness that characterise "Der Hagestolz"
or "Bergkristall." But Stifter's vision is essentially the same in all his fiction: the difference is in *how* he expresses it. In *Witiko* it is the manic
mode that comes to express dimensions of profound otherness, "Unmaß," the unspeakable, even more threateningly and eloquently than
those earlier stories, precisely because he tries to stifle it so completely.

Let us look more closely at the dystopia into which we are transported by this matchless style. In the *Studien, Bunte Steine,* and earlier
Erzählungen, the symbolic landscapes and "spacescapes" are not merely
zones of relative negativity but, as I argued in the case of "Der Hagestolz," of pure "Nichts"; a Nothingness that is not necessarily an emptiness but, rather, a realm of terrifying otherness. The Puszta in
"Brigitta," for example, is a "Nichts" (1,5: 413); Abdias's city has
"keinen Namen . . . keine Bewohner" (1,5: 239); it is "leer," inhabited
by "kein Mensch . . . kein Mensch . . . kein einziger Mensch" (1,5:
266). Furthermore, the function of its derelict walls is "nicht mehr zu

erkennen," for nothing remains but "Stücke, die man gar nicht mehr erkannte" (1,5: 240). Likewise, the European valley has "nicht einmal einen Namen" (1,5: 300).[8] "Bergkristall" is equally threatening: there is initially "nichts zu vernehmen" up on the mountain (2,2: 210); then, later, we read that "hier wurde nichts vernommen; denn hier war nichts zu verkündigen" (2,2: 227).[9] Taken at face value, *Witiko* might appear to be completely different from these stories, seeming as it does to convey an overwhelming sense of positivity and a conviction of existential security. Burger is one of the critics who is clearly happy not to probe beneath the affirmatory surface of this apparently utopian novel when he contrasts what he calls "die radikale Sinnbejahung Stifters" with "die radikale Sinnverneinung Büchners."[10] What probably leads him to view Stifter in such a manner is that the author does indeed present us with an overpowering assurance of positivity that serves on one level to transmit an impression of thereness, of wholeness. This effect is created particularly by the escalating repetition of would-be reassuring phrases such as "es wird gut werden" or "es wird sein." These are evident even in earlier stories such as "Der Waldsteig" (where Maria's father is so convinced that everything will turn out well that he has to say so twice: "es wird schon gut werden . . . , es wird schon alles gut werden," 1,6: 209) and "Granit" (where the old man reassures his young grandson with the words "alles wird gut werden," 2,2: 31); such phrases then come to dominate later works such as *Der Nachsommer* (where Heinrich paces up and down, repeating to himself: "Jetzt ist alles gut, jetzt ist alles gut," *NS* 277, and in which he expresses his conviction that "es wird hier wie überall gut sein," *NS* 389) and "Der fromme Spruch" (in which Dietwin's answer to Gerlint's wish: "Möge es sein, und möge alles gut enden," is an apparently convincing: "Es wird, es wird," *FS* 391; and in which Gerlint confidently states: "Es geht so gut, wie alles nur immer gehen kann," *FS* 372). These assurances, though, begin to ring hollow even in "Granit," when we realise that the grandfather's comforting words are heard only during the pauses in his account of the plague that once devastated the area in which the two characters are cunningly placed. In the later stories, the same words take on further overtones of menace, as they no longer offer even the suggestion of comfort. They become a formula used so relentlessly that it bespeaks not a true conviction of security but a fear, analogous to that embodied in characters such as Abdias, of inexorable disaster. This, surely, is what lies behind the bizarre use of the phrase in the *Letzte Mappe*. Here the topos comes to suggest a world slowly falling apart. There is, for instance, surely something absurd, not to say desperately comic, in the

following conversation between Augustinus and Christine about the missing Eustachius:

> "Aber es hat ja alles gut geendet," antwortete ich.
> "Es hat nicht gut geendet," sagte sie, "und er weiß es." . . .
> "So sind wir einig," sagte sie.
> "Einig, einig," sprach ich. "Wenn nur das letzte Ende dieser Sache gut wird."
> "Es wird gut sein," sagte sie. (*MSB* 94)

A similarly desperate dimension is implied by the conversation between Augustinus and the prince

> "Gebe es Gott, dann kann alles gut werden," sagte ich.
> "Vielleicht nicht alles," erwiderte der Fürst. "Sie werden noch mehr hören."
> Ich schwieg, er sprach sich aber nicht deutlicher aus. (MSB 254)

Again, it is Rosei who is sharp in his perception that Stifter's inclination towards affirmation can be interpreted in a different and far more unsettling manner than traditional criticism would have us believe. He recognises many of the features that I have identified in the narrative mode — and relates them to fear:

> Stifter hat sehr wohl gewußt oder zumindest gespürt, wie dünn das logische, sprachliche Parkett war, auf dem er sich bewegte. Im Alterswerk wird die Angst vor dem Einbrechen in das von Stifter als gesetzlos empfundene "Unten" überdeutlich spürbar. An zahlreichen Stellen sucht er den vorhergegangenen Satz durch den nachfolgenden geradezu zu bestätigen. Die Angst, und es ist keine andere als die alte Angst seines Lebens, zwingt ihn dazu, die Sprache bis auf ihr Skelett abzumagern, die Phantasie bis auf ein Minimum zurückzunehmen und nichts mehr dem "Zufall" zu überlassen. Seine Kunst wird streng affirmativ, hingerichtet auf den Zweck, die Gültigkeit des Ideals zu bestätigen und abzusichern.[11]

Klatt, too, wisely regards the reiterated assurances as no expression of optimism, but as the voice of desperation that is never more desperate than when it cries: "Es wird, es muß ja schließlich alles gut werden."[12]

Although the reiteration of such phrases is indeed a salient feature of the mode employed in the later works as a whole, it is in *Witiko* that their monotonous repetition reverberates most unequivocally with obsession. Here we encounter countless individual characters desperately uttering mantras in order to comfort themselves or others: "es ist gut"; "nun ist alles gut"; "es wird so gut sein"; "es kann gut sein"; "das ist gut"; "mögen die Zeiten immer Gutes bringen"; "es ist Alles gut"; "es ist gut gewesen, wir haben ihn verstanden, und Alles ist gut gewesen,

und ist jetzt gut"; "Alles ist gut geworden"; "das wird sehr gut sein" (5,1: 58, 150, 308; 5,2: 141, 165, 288; 5,3: 101, 137, 230).[13] What is even more disturbing, however, is that we also find whole passages consisting of nothing but these assurances, which gives the eerie impression of an overwhelming *absence* of conviction:

> "[Witiko] hat es gut gemacht, und er ist wie wir, und wir sind wie er. Und es ist Alles gut." [rief Zacharias, der Schenke] . . .
>
> "und es ist gut gewesen, wir haben ihn verstanden, und Alles ist gut gewesen, und ist jetzt gut." [rief Paul Joachim, der Maurer] . . .
>
> "wir können es sagen, daß es nun gut ist." [rief Stephan, der Wagenbauer] (5,3: 101)

As Rosei suggests, this style can convincingly be related to fear. This does not mean that *Witiko* should be interpreted as merely an expression of private neurosis on Stifter's part; nor, of course, should it be related to its setting of twelfth-century Bohemia alone. What the novel most tellingly reflects is the cultural awareness that permeated the whole era in which Stifter wrote — an awareness of the terrifying potential breakdown of all familiar structures; structures that needed desperately to be maintained. Stifter may appear to insist on the cohesive design of his universe by repeating variations on the theme of "es wird sich fügen" in *Witiko*,[14] but the frantic undertone of the refrain expresses only that "the world is out of joint." Like King Canute, Stifter tries in works such as this, "Der fromme Spruch" and the *Letzte Mappe* to ward off the threat of oceanic chaos with his linguistic formulae. However, true to the folk-tale of the ancient king, his enterprise is doomed. But how splendidly doomed! For this mode comes to speak of the tidal wave of collapse which threatens to submerge so many of the fictive characters.

It would be to disambiguate Stifter, however, if I were to maintain that repetition signifies only the fear of the imminent cave-in of all the structures that he cherishes, crucial though this dimension is to his art. Viewed in yet another light, *Witiko* demonstrates a literary style that holds out to the reader a wholly alternative vision; a hidden vision that bespeaks in the most oblique manner the *magnificence* of utter negation. This sense of unappeasable negativity is what Burger evidently, and not surprisingly, fails to perceive when he ascribes such positivity to Stifter's works (whilst also, incidentally, mistakenly imputing unqualified pessimism to those of Büchner). In its style, *Witiko* does indeed present us with an impression of indisputable positivity — but this affirmatory quality of the novel as a whole works in the same manner as Sanna's repeated "Ja Konrad" in "Bergkristall," in that it on one level confirms only the omnipresence of the abyss. The way in which the

characters themselves are conveyed is equally disturbing: by so obsessively asserting the absoluteness of identity, the style of *Witiko* confirms that man's existence, too, is a void. It is again by means of repetition that Stifter seeks to affirm Witiko's identity:

> "Du bist Witiko," sagte Marchard von Hintberg. . . .
> "Du bist Witiko," rief Gebhart von Abbadesorf.
> "Witiko," sagte Viricus von Gaden.
> "Du bist Witiko, und bist noch so jung," sprach Ebergus von Aland. (5,2: 237)

Or:

> "Witiko ist ein Mann," schrie die alte Susanna.
> "'Witiko ist ein Mann," riefen mehrere Mädchen.
> "Ja, er ist es," rief ein alter Bauer. (5,2: 280)

Yet this insistence on the certainty of fixed identity in practice registers a vision similar to the one displayed by the figure of Dall in "Turmalin," according to which man is chaotically fluid, unfixed and indefinable.[15] This is implied even more urgently by the excessive emphasis placed on the word "kennen," which can be seen to carry implications pertaining to identity:

> Der Herzog sprach: "Ihr kennet diesen Mann, und habt ihn schon einmal vor euch gesehen."
> "Wir kennen ihn," sprach Bolemil.
> "Wir kennen ihn," sprach Lubomir.
> "Wir kennen ihn," sprach Otto.
> "Wir kennen ihn," sprach Zdik.
> "Wir kennen ihn," sprachen viele. (5,2: 119)

Witiko himself makes similar claims about Bertha (as, indeed, she does about him):

> "Ich kenne Witiko schon, mein Vater," sagte Bertha.
> "Und ich kenne Bertha," sagte Witiko. (5,3: 123)[16]

In the same manner, Stifter uses repetition in order to assert the validity of traditional absolutes such as honour, truth and fidelity. This is particularly pronounced in the formal manner of the dialogue in which Witiko's proposal to procure Bertha's hand in marriage is accepted:

> "ich, Witiko vom Witikohause, ein Herr im mittäglichen Böhmen unter dem erlauchten Herzoge von Böhmen und Mähren, Wladislaw, werbe in Gutem und Treuem um eure Tochter, das tugendreiche Fräulein Bertha, daß sie mir in freiem Willen als Ehegemahlin folge, und daß ich sie ehre und liebe und ihr treu bin, so lange ich lebe. Ich bitte euch um eine Antwort auf meine Werbung."

Heinrich von Schauenberg stand auf, und sprach: "Witiko vom Witikohause, Herr im mittäglichen Böhmen unter dem Herzoge Wladislaw, ich, Heinrich von Schauenberg, gebe dir in Gutem und Treuem meine Tochter Bertha, daß sie dir in freiem Willen als Ehegemahlin folge, daß du sie ehrest und liebest, und ihr treu bist, so lange du lebst, und daß sie dich ehret und liebt und dir treu ist, so lange sie lebt. Hier ist Wiulfhilt von Dornberg, meine Gemahlin, hier ist Werinhart von Jugelbach, mein Vater, hier ist Benedicta von Aschach, meine Mutter, hier ist Gebhart von Stauf, mein Bruder. Sie sagen, daß die Ehre der Werbung gepflogen ist, und daß Bertha in deinem Stamme ist, wie in unserem Stamme."

Wiulfhilt stand auf, und sprach: "Die Ehre ist gepflogen, und Bertha ist in Witiko's Stamme wie in unserem Stamme.'

Werinhart stand auf, und sprach: "Die Ehre ist gepflogen, und Bertha ist in Witiko's Stamme wie in unserem Stamme."

Und Benedicta stand auf, und sprach: "Die Ehre ist gepflogen, und Bertha ist in Witiko's Stamme wie in unserem Stamme."

Und Gebhart von Stauf stand auf, und sprach: "Die Ehre ist gepflogen, und Bertha ist in Witiko's Stamme wie in unserem Stamme."

Nun sprach Heinrich von Schauenberg: "So sage Bertha, daß sie in freiem Willen der Werbung folge, oder daß sie in freiem Willen die Werbung nicht annehme." . . .

Heinrich von Schauenberg sprach: "Bertha von Schauenberg, Tochter Heinrichs und Wiulfhilts, hier steht Witiko vom Witikohause, ein Herr im mittäglichen Böhmen unter dem Herzoge Wladislaw, und wirbt in Gutem und Treuem, daß du ihm in freiem Willen als Ehegemahlin folgest, und ihn ehrest und liebst und ihm treu bist, so lange du lebst, und daß er dich ehret und liebt und dir treu ist, so lange er lebt. Gib ihm eine Antwort."

Bertha sprach: "Ich, Bertha von Schauenberg, die Tochter Heinrichs und Wiulfhilts, werde in freiem Willen Witiko vom Witikohause, dem Herrn im mittäglichen Böhmen unter dem Herzoge Wladislaw als Ehegemahlin folgen, daß ich ihn ehre und liebe und ihm treu bin, so lange ich lebe." (5,3: 198–9)

The words to which our attention is drawn are those such as "das Gute," "das Treue," "Tugend," "Ehre," and "Liebe," all of which possess overwhelmingly positive connotations. Yet the repetition of these terms upon which so many social structures are still based does not, as Rupp would have it, suggest "sociability" or "courtesy"[17]: it comes across as nothing so much as an obsessive ritual. This is a style that begins to turn in upon itself, as it were, undermining these key concepts by the very act of excessively emphasising them — and rendering thereby a vision of the amoral splendour of the void. The novel's manic emphasis on "Ordnung"[18] and "Mäßigung"[19] works in the same way, as

does the obsessive repetition of "Recht," "das Rechte," "es wird recht werden"[20] — a topos that the dialogue once again displays particularly effectively:

> [Witiko sagte] "Alles wird recht sein."
> "Es wird schon recht sein," sagte David, der Zimmerer.
> "Und ich werde auch schon machen, daß es recht ist," sagte der Schmied. . . .
> "Und ich werde es noch besser machen," sagte Tom Johannes der Fiedler. (5,2: 297)

The manic repetition of the formula again signifies the magnificent chaos of the underlying abyss beyond order or measure, where nothing can come good, nothing can come right.

Bearing in mind that such concepts also carry a religious significance of which Stifter would have been fully aware, I should perhaps cast a glance at the implications that the author's later style has concerning his attitude to "things." As I noted earlier in the case of the *Letzte Mappe*, the manic manner in which he uses the verb "sein" ultimately expresses the absence of any divine meaning in "things," no matter how much they may be revered. In the case of *Witiko*, the same lack of inherent meaning is registered by the way that the characters are made to chant the phrase "Es ist so": "'So ist es, wie es ist,' sagte Heinrich"; "'So ist es,' sagte Silvester"; "'Ja, ja, so ist es,' sagte Huldrik . . . 'Ja, so ist es, so ist es'"; "'Ja, so ist es,' rief Tom Johannes . . . 'So ist es,' rief eine Stimme"; "'So ist es gut, und so thun wir,' sagte Rowno. 'Wir thun so,' sagte Diet. 'So thun wir,' riefen alle" (5,1: 47, 152, 227, 266, 268); "'So ist es,' 'so soll es immer sein,' 'gedenkt es,' 'so ist es,' 'so ist es,' 'so thut es,' riefen mehrere Stimmen durcheinander"; "'So ist es,' entgegnete Zdik" (5,2: 79, 175); "'Ich weiß, daß es so ist,' sprach die Base"; "'So ist es,' entgegnete Zdik"; "'So ist es,' riefen viele Männer"; "'Es ist so,' 'ja so ist es,' 'so ist es,' riefen viele Männer" "'So ist es, so ist es,' riefen mehrere Männer" (5,3: 90, 173, 262, 304, 305). Far from upholding the existential security with which it purports to present us, the mania inherent in this mode of writing again suggests a negative: "Es ist *nicht* so." And the more insistent the assertions become, the more the style embraces the zone of the negative:

> Guido, der Kardinal [sprach]: "Zdik, hochehrwürdiger Bischof von Olmüz, Bischof des Landes Mähren, die Sprossen des hohen Stammes Přemysl, welche gegen die Kirche in Mähren und gegen dich gefehlt haben, sind des Fehls geständig und reuig, und haben auf das Kreuz des Heilandes geschworen, der Kirche und dir die völlige Genugthuung zu leisten. Ist es nicht so? Ich bitte dich, Konrad, rede."
> "Es ist so," sagte Konrad. . . .

"Es ist so," sagte Wratislaw. . . .
"Es ist so," sagte Otto. (5,3: 157)[21]

Surely this is not merely a demonstration of pathological anxiety that it is "nicht so," nor even an example of a style that allows negativity to express itself through the many lacunae in its affirmatory surface. It is in one sense a mode whereby linguistic positivity confirms and even marvels at the unfathomable negativity of the void. The form of the novel is one hugely affirmative "Ja, ja, ja" (5,3: 264)[22] — but it is this that also signifies the ultimate in a vision of negativity. That we are taken into a void zone in which all the boundaries of fixed time are burst is made clear by the use of different tenses in the formula. Thus we find a litany of phrases that refer to the past, present and future: "alles ist gut geworden" (5,3: 137); "jetzt ist Alles gut, jetzt hat Gott mein Gebet erhört, wir wissen es, und wissen schon Alles, es ist Alles gut" (5,3: 135); "die Zukunft wird sich erfüllen" (5,3: 178); "es wird so gut sein" (5,1: 308).[23] In this way, a layer of the style bespeaks the same measureless infinitude as that which characterises so many of the infinitely negative symbolic locations conjured up by Stifter with such force in his earlier stories.

Of course, these locations are characterised as much by their *silence* as by their infinitude. This is one of the most crucial aspects of Stifter's work, for what is conveyed is no ordinary silence: it is the terrible silence of the void. Again, this is made explicit in the evocations of the fictive terrain in the earlier stories. The silence of the African desert in "Abdias," for example, is penetrated only by the noise of predatory animals (1,5: 242); that of the heath in "Das Haidedorf" is broken by nothing more than the terrified cry of a victim of one of those predators ("Angstschrei des Kibitz," 1,4: 203); the two children in the inset story in "Granit" find themselves in a forest that is utterly silent apart from "der Schrei eines wilden Thieres" (2,2: 54). The trees in the Major's garden in "Brigitta" are "todesstille" (1,5: 422), and the silence of the forest in "Die Mappe" is likewise "[eine] Todtenstille" (1,5: 96). Even more terrifying is "Bergkristall," in which the narrator impassively reports: "Es war große Ruhe eingetreten. Von den Vögeln . . . war nichts zu vernehmen . . . , und der ganze Wald war gleichsam ausgestorben" (2,2: 210); a vision that recurs with even more telling effect as late as *Der Nachsommer*, in which not merely the forest but the whole of the earth seems to have died out: "Alles schwieg unter mir, als wäre die Welt ausgestorben" (*NS* 423; both of these, of course, clearly echo the "Rings ausgestorbene Stille" experienced by Cornelia in "Der Condor," 1,4: 23). Such silences are entirely absent from the surface of texts such as "Der fromme Spruch," "Der Kuß von Sentze," *Witiko*, and the

Letzte Mappe. However, Stifter's medium again becomes his message in these later stories. As I observed earlier, for example, the mode in certain parts of the *Letzte Mappe* purports to offer full explanations of events, but the "explanations" suggest only portentous emptiness. The more Anna repeats her assurances, the more empty her words become until she finally declares: "es wird schon werden . . . Es wird schon gut werden . . . Es soll so sein" (*MSB* 214). This is the style in which the later Stifter excels, and it characterises both *Der Nachsommer* ('Eustach . . . [pflegte] auch zu sagen . . . , das Gute sei gut, weil es gut sei," *NS* 543) and "Der fromme Spruch" ("Der Oheim sprach: 'Das ist nun freilich anders, als wir gedacht haben, wir müssen es hinnehmen, daß wir gedacht haben, was wir gedacht haben,'" *FS* 450). The conversation in the *Letzte Mappe* between Augustinus and the villager about whether or not to summon a doctor can be viewed in the same way. In *Witiko*, however, this style does not only govern particular passages: the form of the whole novel registers the silence of the abyss. This is most graphic in the manner in which the characters' speech — and speech that, incidentally, constitutes over two thirds of the novel — constantly conveys nothing.[24] The ritual conversations are dominated by utterances such as: "was gethan werden muß, das wird gethan werden"; "es geschehe, was geschehen muß"; "So ist gesprochen, was zuerst gesprochen werden sollte"; "Und so ist nun erfüllet, was erfüllt werden sollte"; "Du bist mir lieb gewesen, weil du mir lieb gewesen bist" (5,2: 319, 292; 5,3: 121, 122, 126). This form reaches a peak in the middle of the scene in which Witiko and Bertha declare their feelings for one another:

> "Und wenn ich heute nicht gekommen wäre," sprach Witiko.
> "So wärest du später gekommen," sagte Bertha.
> "Und wenn ich gar nicht gekommen wäre," sprach Witiko.
> "Das ist nicht möglich," sagte Bertha, "weil du gekommen bist."
>
> (5,3: 127)

This style even dominates the narrator's account of the events, when he comments: "es wurde gesprochen, was in Plan gesprochen worden war" (5,3: 105). Here, the medium is again the message — and it intimates something far beyond the mutual security that I detected in the phatic conversations portrayed in "Der fromme Spruch." *Witiko* is one enormous word-litany: it is a mirage of substance which simultaneously reveals its essential nothingness, indeed Nothingness as an absolute. The "silence" registered by the style is the same as that which characterises the old man's island in *Der Hagestolz* where God has long since been dead and gone, which is beyond the peal of the church bells on the mainland; or the one that characterises the mountain in "Bergkristall"

that, again, the church bells cannot penetrate. The language that Stifter heaps up is full of sound and fury, signifying nothing — and this does not indicate a failure on the author's part to convey his "meaning." On the contrary, this style conveys just as fully as (and even more grippingly than) the content the hidden, manic dimensions of the work. The novel is marked by bizarrely empty conversations such as those held between Witiko and Huldrik (conversations which yet again prefigure twentieth-century Absurdism). The hero's first conversation with Huldrik is as portentously empty as Anna's "explanation":

> Huldrik [sprach]: "Es gehen alle Zeichen in Erfüllung, und es wird wahr, was die alten Leute gesagt haben, daß es wahr werden soll, und es ist wahr, wie sie gesagt haben, daß es gewesen ist."
> "Nun, was haben sie denn gesagt?" fragte Witiko.
> "Ihr wißt es ja ohnehin," sagte Huldrik.
> "Ich weiß es nicht," entgegnete Witiko.
> "So hätten sie es euch sagen sollen . . . ," erwiederte Huldrik.
> (5,1: 228)

His subsequent encounter with Huldrik is no less bizarre:

> "Ich sage es dir, Huldrik," antwortete Witiko, " . . . wie noch Alles wird, ist in Gottes Hand."
> "Es wird, es wird," sagte Huldrik. "Und wenn es doch wäre, daß es nicht würde, dann, dann."
> "Was dann?" fragte Witiko. (5,3: 99–100)

He may well ask. His conversation with an anonymous door-keeper is of the same proto-Absurd order:

> Und als Witiko das Pferd wie gewöhnlich bedeckt hatte, sagte er: "Nun führe mich in die Stube."
> "In die Stube, in die Stube," sagte der alte Mann. (5,1: 223)

Yet it is hardly relevant to complain that Stifter's peasants "do not speak as we would expect peasants to speak,"[25] for this mode of writing is an expression of the silence of the unspeakable: it signifies the zone of otherness in which there is "nichts zu verkündigen" that is so terrifying in "Bergkristall" (2,2: 27). Again, this kind of style is prefigured as early as 1850 in "Der beschriebene Tännling." The most striking dialogue in this story reads as follows:

> Es ward in dem Saale etwas stiller, und der Herr las mit lauter Stimme aus einem Papiere vor: "Herr Andreas bei der rothen Lake."
> "Weiß sie nicht."
> "Gidi wird dich führen."
> "Herr Gunibald in der Kreixe."
> "Weiß sie."

> "Herr Friedrich von Eschberg am gebrannten Steine."
> "Weiß ihn nicht"
> "Der Schmied Feirer wird euch begleiten."
> "Herr Guido beim beschriebenen Tännling."
> "Weiß ihn."
> "Herr Albrecht Hammermann im Fuchslug."
> "Weiß es."
> "Herr Thorngar am Brunnkreß — Herr Wenhard am Obergehag — Herr Emerich im Auwörth."
> "Wissen es."
> Und so ging es fort (1,6: 422)

Again, this tells us that *Witiko* cannot be divorced from Stifter's other creations — but what makes the novel unique is the sheer *volume* of the words. These words are not a precarious means by which to suppress the silence of the abyss: it is precisely their volume that expresses this silence. This is perhaps most startling in the way in which the characters are made almost to chant their phrases at formal meetings:

> "Ich habe die Worte gehört," sprach Zwest.
> "Ich habe die Worte gehört," sprach Wecel.
> "Ich habe die Worte gehört," sprach Zdeslaw.
> "Ich habe die Worte gehört," sprach Bohuslaw.
> "Ich habe die Worte gehört," sprach Casta. . . .
> "Und sprechen die andern Männer auch, daß Konrad, der Herzog von Znaim, die Worte gesagt hat?" fragte der Herzog Wladislaw.
> "Er hat sie gesagt," sprach Zwest.
> "Er hat sie gesagt," sprach Wecel.
> "Er hat sie gesagt," sprach Zdeslaw.
> "Er hat sie gesagt," sprach Bohuslaw.
> "Er hat sie gesagt," sprach Casta. (5,2: 316–17)

This mode escalates as the novel reaches its close, where we find in quick succession the following exchanges:

> "So sind wir fertig," sprach der Kaiser. "Hochwürdiger Erzbischof von Mainz, wie nennt man das, was Mailand übt?"
> "Empörung," sagte der Erzbischof.
> "Und du von Köln?" fragte der Kaiser.
> "Empörung," antwortete der Erzbischof von Köln.
> "Und du von Trier?" fragte der Kaiser.
> "Empörung," antwortete der Erzbischof von Trier.
> "Und ihr andern?" fragte der Kaiser.
> "Empörung," riefen alle. (5,3: 288–9)

> "Ich schwimme mit," rief Mathias.
> "Ich schwimme mit," rief Urban.

"Ich schwimme mit," rief Maz Albrecht.
"Ich schwimme mit," rief Wolf. . . .
"Ich schwimme mit," rief Augustin.
"Ich schwimme mit, ich schwimme mit," riefen alle Männer.

(5,3: 292–3)

"Und was ist die Folge des Beschlusses?" fragte der Kaiser.
"Der Bann," sagte der Erzbischof von Mainz.
"Der Bann," sagte der Erzbischof von Trier.
"Der Bann," sagte der Erzbischof von Köln.
"Der Bann," sagten die Herzoge und Bischöfe und Fürsten.

(5,3: 305)[26]

In these instances, even the typography of the novel is eloquent: in ways
not possible with less stylised dialogue the words on the page evoke the
refrain-like recurrence of silence, of blank paper, of void. *Witiko* is a
Something that is far more disturbing than a Nothing. For all its wordi-
ness, it presents us with powerfully wordless images of possibilities
which remain unspoken because they are unspeakable. This manner of
writing is a *Sinnbild* in exactly the same way as are the characters' collections or the landscapes in which they are placed. Like these, it is a
signifier that can signify any number of "layers" or "strands" of Stifter's
creativity: in *Witiko* it signifies in a crucial sense the ineffable, a Something that cannot even be conceptualised. The novel's words dance
around the abyss, uttering one prolonged, silent scream. We are confronted with a style that is perhaps too radical to be fully appreciated
even today, not to mention in 1864. It is just as far off the map as the
uncle's island in "Der Hagestolz" or the upper reaches of the mountain
in "Bergkristall." Stifter bursts the boundaries of stylistic convention in
Witiko, giving us a linguistic otherness "so außerordentlich, wie es gar
nicht auszusprechen ist" (*NS* 650). This, as Rosei suggests, is not
merely an attempt to bridge the void, but a form of writing that comes
from within that very abyss, as it were. The novel is written in the realm
of the "Nichts," in the "Jenseits" that has ceased to exist.[27]

Witiko is perhaps the most fascinating of Stifter's works for various
reasons. It may be that Barnes is right to see it as an interesting failure,
"a regrettable experiment, in which an ageing author showed himself
both mannered and verbose."[28] But I suggest that in truth it is his
manic masterpiece, the most compelling expression of a vision of fracture, and chaos beyond all measure and moderation. It is interesting to
note that critics are very slowly beginning to take account of the
novel — and it is particularly pleasing to see that Matz recently commented on its modern appeal. He echoes Rosei when he argues of
Stifter:

paradoxerweise nähert sich seine karge, bis ins Extrem reduzierte Sprache damit eher Prosaformen des 20. Jahrhunderts als den imaginären historischen Vorbildern.

> Modern ist all das am *Witiko*, was die Zeitgenossen so verstörte: die bis auf ihr Skelett abgemagerte Sprache, der emotionslose Protokollstil, die fast leblose Abstraktheit der Gestalten.[29]

Of course, this is only a tentative start, and the novel largely remains an enigma, its depths scarcely fathomed or even perceived. Stifter himself was clearly pleased with this work into which he claimed to have poured his "Herzblut" (*Briefe*, 407), for he uncharacteristically never made any attempt to rewrite it. Whether one chooses to view the novel as a failure or a success — or even as simply unreadable — it has to be seen in the context of the whole Biedermeier era that, far from being stable, was crumbling around its denizens' ears. Stifter is all too aware of the insidious disintegration of everything dear to him, and obsessively tries to conjure up security through the medium of his prose. The proleptic statements uttered by the characters in *Witiko* such as: "so siehe, wie die Sache ist . . . aber beeile dich, es könnte bald alles anders werden" (5,2: 21), or "alles kann jetzt anders sein, es kann auch so sein, wie es gewesen ist, wir wissen es nicht" (5,2: 295–6) accordingly have a resonance far beyond twelfth-century Bohemia. Fischer is aware of this dimension to the author's fiction: "Stifter ist ein scharfsinniger, weitsichtiger und rücksichtsloser Zeitkritiker, der zwar den offenen Kampf meidet, aber abständig das Unerhörte sagt."[30] Like his acquaintance Anton Bruckner (leader of the music at his funeral),[31] Adalbert Stifter was a Biedermeier backwoodsman who nonetheless magisterially transcended not only the limitations of his own personal background and horizons, but also the artistic conventions and fashions of his age, in order to voice a profoundly modern vision that is only now beginning to be truly appreciated.

Notes

[1] Peter Rosei, "Versuch über Stifter und einige Schriftsteller der Gegenwart," *Literatur und Kritik*, 103 (1976): 166.

[2] Mann, *Briefe*, 458.

[3] Matz, unsurprisingly, overlooks the significance of the story's dialogue. He is right to say that there is not much of it — but wrong to say that it plays no role (*Adalbert Stifter*, 241–2).

[4] We find a similar repetition later on (5,3: 312). Significantly, this style comes more and more to dominate in the novel. See, for example, the repetitions of "nannte" (5,3: 180); "standen" (5,3: 182); "folgten" (5,3: 183).

[5] Wildbolz, *Langeweile und Faszination*, 17.

[6] Wildbolz, *Langeweile und Faszination*, 140.

[7] Wildbolz, *Langeweile und Faszination*, 122.

[8] See Helena Ragg-Kirkby, "'So ward die Wüste immer größer:' Zones of Otherness in the Stories of Adalbert Stifter," *Forum for Modern Language Studies* 35 (1999): 207–22.

[9] This sentence has attracted critical attention. Stopp argues that "hier war nichts zu verkündigen, denn von hier ging durch die Kinder eine Verkündigung aus" (Frederick J. Stopp, "Die Symbolik in Stifters *Bunten Steinen*," *Deutsche Vierteljahresschrift für Literatur und Geistesgeschichte*, 28 [1954]: 177). Irmscher comments: "Das soll doch wohl heißen: hier war Gott selbst gegenwärtig" (*Wirklichkeitserfahrung und gegenständliche Darstellung*, 249). These, however are contorted (not to say casuistical) interpretations that turn the textual evidence upside down.

[10] Burger, "Der Stilwille der Unzeitgemäßen," 295.

[11] Rosei, "Versuch über Stifter," 167.

[12] Klatt, "Stifter und das Dämonische," 279.

[13] Phrases of this kind are repeated with astonishing frequency in various forms ("es ist gut," "alles ist gut," "es ist alles gut," "die Sache ist sehr gut," "da wird alles gut werden" etc.). See, for example, 5,1: 52, 103, 180, 187, 192, 204, 218, 226, 246, 301; 5,2: 86, 93, 109, 228, 232, 304, 305, 322; 5,3: 58, 103, 260, 262.

[14] Again, this phrase recurs with slight variations ("es wird sich fügen," "wie es sich fügt," "Gott kann Alles fügen," "es könnte sich fügen," etc.). See, for example, 5,1: 172, 177, 224, 230; 5,2: 108, 135, 143, 145, 158, 166, 242, 246, 249, 264, 301, 319; 5,3: 113, 202–3.

[15] This limitless fluidity and absolute lack of fixed identity is particularly clearly implied in the description of the Major and his love affairs in "Brigitta": "Mit aller Lieblichkeit, die ihm jedes Herz gewann und das der Erkornen mit siegreicher Wonne füllte, benahm er sich bis zu Ende, dann nahm er Abschied, machte eine Reise, und kam nicht wieder"; "es sei noch niemanden . . . gelungen, ihn länger zu fesseln, als es ihm eben beliebte" (1,5: 414). The word "fesseln" is also used in "Turmalin" in the context of Dall who, like the Major, cannot be pinned down in any way: "Man suchte ihn, und bestrebte sich, ihn zu feßeln" (2,2: 141). Dall is one of the most disturbing characters ever created by Stifter. It is clear in the book version that he has no identity beyond the stage door (2,2: 140). It seems, therefore, no coincidence that the actor or "role player" has his own "Rollstuhl" in his acquaintance's apartment. The words "roll" / "rollen" / "Rollen" occur five times in the space of one paragraph about the furniture (in the sense of "roll," 2,2: 136), and then "Rolle(n)" occurs a further five times in the seemingly objective account of Dall as a character (in the sense of "role," 2,2: 139–40). It is interesting to note that this word appears only once in the journal version, and in a different context: "Diese Künstlerpersönlichkeit spielte eine Rolle in unserer Geschichte" (2,1: 115). Such signs point in a sinister direction to a realm beyond identity: a realm in which the rooms are a symbolic representation of what is profoundly and shockingly unknowable in humans. Perhaps the most disturbing thing about it is that it suggests that all humans simply play roles, wear masks (this is also reminiscent of *Dantons Tod*). Stifter would never have dreamed of writing "Jeder Mensch ist ein Abgrund" (Büchner, *Sämtliche Werke*, vol. 1, 377) — but this is what he constantly implies.

[16] Once the notion of fixed identity has been shaken in such a way, statements such as "Witiko kann ja nicht anders sein als er ist" (5,3: 93) come across to the reader as desperate attempts to uphold something that has already fallen down.

[17] Rupp, *Stifters Sprache*, 84.

[18] Order is emphasised in *Witiko* perhaps more insistently than in any other of Stifter's stories. It is constantly asserted at the Assemblies ("Die Ordnung der Versammlung," 5,1: 119, 126) and people speak in order, walk in order, act in order, order their possessions, order their thoughts, order themselves. See, for example, 5,1: 115, 132, 140, 166, 171, 286, 289; 5,2: 46, 47, 48, 73, 79, 93, 119, 177, 182, 195, 279, 297, 298, 322, 323; 5,3: 12, 18, 27, 64, 71, 110, 142, 191, 192, 193, 214, 215, 228, 254. Obviously this is not a complete list of every reference to "Ordnung," "ordnen," and "geordnet," but it nonetheless demonstrates the astounding frequency with which the words are used.

[19] Like order, moderation is claimed as one of the strengths of the Assemblies: "Die Kraft einer jeden Versammlung ist ihre Mäßigung" (5,1: 126);

"Halten wir die Kraft und die Gerechtigkeit und die Mäßigkeit aufrecht, daß aus dem Bösen das Gute werde" (5,3: 238). Again, however, the words "Mäßigkeit" and "Mäßigung" do not create moderation. On the contrary: the very insistence on these words itself becomes the most eloquent expression of mania.

[20] "Recht" is repeated in various forms even more obsessively than "Ordnung." "Es wird recht werden" and "es ist recht" are two of the most frequently recurring phrases in the text. For these and very similar phrases see, for example, 5,1: 51, 169, 179, 262, 265, 310; 5,2: 48, 227, 297, 298, 311, 322; 5,3: 58, 75, 137. The words "Recht" and "das Rechte" occur even more frequently: see, for example, 5,1: 250, 251, 256, 260, 302; 5,2: 17, 21, 39, 40, 118, 121, 133, 134, 145, 150, 151, 233, 236, 249, 276, 311; 5,3: 37, 42, 51, 143, 145, 151, 152, 227, 237, 238, 258, 262, 264, 286, 329, 330. Again, this is by no means a complete list.

[21] See also 5,1: 226, 258; 5,2: 81, 146, 150, 214, 229, 304, 322; 5,3: 24, 156, 157, 227, 241, 260, 264.

[22] This is constantly repeated — along with its opposite: "Ja, ja, ja" (5,3: 264); "Nein, nein, nein" (5,3: 264); "Ja, ja, ja, ja" (5,1: 146); "Nein, nein, nein" (5,1: 146); "ja, ja" (5,1: 136); "Ja, ja . . . Ja, ja, ja . . . Ja . . . Ja, ja" (5,1: 137); "Ja, ja" (5,1: 172); "Ja, ja . . . Ja, ja" (5,1: 246); "Ja, ja, ja" (5,2: 109). The same obsessive positivity is found in "Der fromme Spruch": "'Ja, ja, ja,' sagte die Tante" (*FS* 451).

[23] See 5,1: 95, 160, 185, 211, 226, 230, 303; 5,2: 38, 181, 195, 264; 5,3: 241.

[24] Risach reports: "Mathilde und ich sprachen gewöhnliche Dinge, und in den gewöhnlichen Dingen lag ein Sinn, den wir verstanden" (*NS* 652). Despite his protestations, though, the "Sinn" evades the the reader.

[25] Branscombe, "Some Reflections on the Use of Dialogue," 13.

[26] It is interesting to note that the layout of Stifter's painting diary is the same as the manuscript of *Witiko*: the repetitions are not signified by any kind of shorthand but are all written out in full (extracts from both are reproduced in Roedl, *Stifter in Selbstzeugnissen und Bilddokumenten*, 114, 124).

[27] This image is, of course, taken from "Bergkristall": "Jenseits wollten [die Kinder] wieder hinabklettern. Aber es gab kein Jenseits" (2,2: 220).

[28] Barnes, "The Function of Conversations and Speeches in *Witiko*," 2.

[29] Matz, *Adalbert Stifter*, 367.

[30] Fischer, "Versuch der Verständigung. Gedanken und Deutungen im Anschluß an Adalbert Stifters *Zuversicht*," *VASILO*, 9 (1960): 96.

[31] The symmetry between Stifter and Bruckner as artistic phenomena is extraordinary and can scarcely be coincidental. *Mutatis mutandis*, we might as well be reading a traditional critique of Stifter when we read of Bruckner:

"There is a certain naïvety in his work, and a lack of adroitness in contrivance (particularly an amount of repetition of phrases perhaps beyond that of any other composer whatever)." Percy A. Scholes, *The Oxford Companion to Music*, ed. John Owen Ward (Oxford: Oxford UP, 1992; first published 1938), 138.

Conclusion

AT THE START OF THIS BOOK, I aligned myself unequivocally with the "new wave" of Stifter criticism: those commentators who detect realms of mania beneath the smooth, unruffled surfaces of the texts. However, their arguments are as much a matter of perspective as are the claims of the critics who seek to uphold the traditional picture of Stifter. What I suggest is that both voices have to be heard: moderation and mania cannot exist without one another in Stifter's fiction, and it is only because the latter is so obsessively unruffled, balanced, measured that it becomes so threateningly manic. This split perspective of measure and mania is given vivid expression in texts such as "Der Condor" and "Der Hochwald," and so critics have tended to concentrate on these and similar texts of Stifter's early and middle periods. They perhaps assume that, because the later texts do not thematise dual perspectives in this way, the abyss has somehow been bridged or left behind. But this later prose expresses exactly the same problems in its *form*. Here, the medium becomes the message — and its extreme moderation is the most extraordinary and extreme mania. This is precisely what happens in *Witiko*, which is long overdue for recognition as one of the most significant and daring novels of the nineteenth century. For all its apparent conformity, *Witiko* offers us absolute nonconformity in style; it displays cadences and rhythms of truth achieved and simultaneously exploded, and any analysis of Stifter's fiction that ignores the novel can be nowhere near complete. There is no doubt that the themes around which he builds his earlier stories are enormously revealing — but they provide only half the picture: the other half lies in the way that his style becomes so radically other and ultimately dissolves into the kind of extreme obliqueness that will only be anywhere near matched almost a century later by Beckett or Ionesco. It is interesting to note that, even during the last couple of years, critics have not fully tuned in to this. Matz, in the most recent Stifter biography (1995), is generally very alive to the turmoil beneath the smooth surface — but his comment on "Prokopus" illustrates the extent to which Stifter's modernism is still largely overlooked:

> Die Novelle liest sich wie eine lange Einleitung zu einer Novelle, die niemals beginnt. Damit ist sie indessen ein getreues Abbild der Geschichte, von der sie berichtet — ein *allzu* getreues. Das endlose

Warten auf etwas, was niemals kommt, das kann wohl der Gehalt eines Lebens und auch der einer Erzählung sein, nicht aber das Formprinzip des Textes selber.[1]

One cannot help wondering what Matz's view of *Waiting for Godot* might be.

This brings me to the second point at which I diverge even from the generality of "new" critics. The vast majority of Stifter's critics, both those who read his fiction with the grain and those who read it against the grain, have tended to see Stifter as a natural heir to the great Classical tradition — as he indeed saw himself (in one of his more immodest moments, he compared his written correspondence with Heckenast to that between Goethe and Schiller[2]). But I hope to have demonstrated that he is at the same time a torchbearer, however unwillingly, for the most powerful and characteristic tendencies within modernist literature. He opens a Pandora's box and, however hard he tries, he cannot close the lid again. He is irretrievably spreadeagled between a comforting faith in divine order and human reason, and a terrifying vision of infinite emptiness and futility. In this way he differs from authors such as Kleist, who aspire to enter paradise through the back door, as it were. Stifter asserts a surface paradise of Biedermeier gentility — but beneath it is the same absurdity and potential terror that famously characterise Kafka's work.

This book makes no claim to be a comprehensive answer to the challenge posed by Stifter's fiction; indeed, the more one reads Stifter's works, the more beautifully elusive they become. I am putting forward a *perspective*: a new and hopefully revealing way of looking at the oeuvre (or, in the case of *Witiko*, perhaps even listening to it). This, of course, is true to the nature of Stifter's writing. It would perhaps be easy to assume that an author like Stifter who constantly puts forward his uncompromisingly "moral" opinions in matters of religion, art, nature, meaning, and truth might leave little open to the critic (and this may well account for the tendency even among modern readers to dismiss him out of hand). But what the texts offer in practice is a bewildering array of interpretations and perspectives — and these are themselves perhaps the most eloquent tokens of Stifter's hidden vision of fragmentation and chaos. The critic, meanwhile, is left to offer perspectives on Stifter's multiple perspectives. For example, whilst I have suggested that the mode employed by the later Stifter comes to evoke an existence devoid of meaning, cohesion and wholeness, we must remember that, on another level — and a quite profound one — there *is* absolute measure, order, wholeness in the world as he perceives it. Again, these

are both interpretations — and, as Kafka's prison chaplain warns Josef K. in *Der Prozeß*:

> Du mußt nicht zuviel auf Meinungen achten. Die Schrift ist unveränderlich und die Meinungen sind oft nur ein Ausdruck der Verzweiflung darüber.[3]

Notes

[1] Matz, *Adalbert Stifter*, 261; his emphasis.

[2] *Briefe*, 259, 262; *MSB* 727, 842.

[3] Franz Kafka, *Der Prozeß*, in Franz Kafka, *Gesammelte Werke*, ed. Max Brod [Frankfurt am Main]: Fischer, 1965, 260.

Bibliography

Works by Adalbert Stifter

Säm(m)tliche Werke. Ed. August Sauer, Franz Hüller, Kamill Eben, and Gustav Wilhelm. Prague: J. G. Calve; Reichenberg: Franz Kraus; Graz: Stiasnh, 1901–60.

Briefe. Ed. Hans Schumacher. Zurich: Manesse, 1947.

Gesammelte Werke in sechs Bänden. Frankfurt am Main: Insel, 1959.

"Der fromme Spruch." In *Gesammelte Werke in vierzehn Bänden*. Ed. Konrad Steffen. Basel and Stuttgart: Birkhäuser, 1964, vol. 5.

Die Mappe meines Urgroßvaters. Schilderungen. Briefe. Munich: Winkler, 1968.

Der Nachsommer. Munich: Winkler, 1978.

"Der Hochwald." Ed. Emil Merker. Stuttgart: Reclam, 1998.

Werke und Briefe. Historisch-kritische Gesamtausgabe. Ed. Alfred Doppler and Wolfgang Frühwald. Stuttgart, Berlin, Cologne, and Mainz: Kohlhammer, 1978–.

Works Consulted

Adorno, Theodor W. "Über epische Naivetät." In Theodor W. Adorno. *Noten zur Literatur*. Frankfurt am Main: Suhrkamp, 1958, vol 1.

Amann, Klaus. "Zwei Thesen zu Stifters *Nachsommer*." *VASILO* 31 (1982): 169–84.

Anon. [various titles] *VASILO* 1 *et seq* 1952– : a round-up of secondary literature is published in almost all issues of the periodical under varying titles, e.g. "Literatur-Mosaik," "Dissertationen über Adalbert Stifter," "Von kommenden Stifterbüchern," "Instituts-Bibliothek," "Presse-Echo."

——. "Adalbert-Stifter-Bibliographie 1988–1990 mit Nachträgen," *VASILO* 39 (1990), 3/4: 41–69.

Appuhn-Radtke, Sibylle. "'Priester des Schönen:' Adalbert Stifters Künstler-bild zwischen theoretischem Anspruch, literarischer Darstellung und gesellschaftlicher Realität." In *Adalbert Stifter: Dichter und Maler, Denk-malpfleger und Schulmann. Neue Zugänge zu seinem Werk.* Ed. Hartmut Laufhütte and Karl Möseneder. Tübingen: Niemeyer, 1996, 75–95.

Aprent, Johann. *Adalbert Stifter.* Ed. Moriz Enzinger. Nuremberg: Hans Carl, 1955.

Aspetsberger, Friedrich. "Stifters Tautologien." *VASILO* 15 (1966): 23–44.

——. "Der Groß-Sprecher Heinrich Drendorf: Zu Adalbert Stifters *Nach-sommer.*" *VASILO* 32 (1983): 197–219.

Augustin, Hermann. "Ärztliches zu Adalbert Stifters Tod." *VASILO* 8 (1959), 19–34.

Bandet, Jean-Louis. "Livres sur Adalbert Stifter," *Études germaniques* 24 (1969): 562–6.

——. "Les chiffres de la solitude." *Études germaniques* 40 (1985): 271–80.

Barnes, H. G. "The Function of Conversations and Speeches in *Witiko.*" In *German Studies Presented to H. G. Fiedler.* Oxford: Oxford UP, 1938, 1–25.

Beckmann, Martin. "Die ästhetische Funktion des Weg-Motivs in Stifters *Nachsommer.*" *VASILO* 39 (1990) 3/4: 3–23.

Begemann, Christian. *Die Welt der Zeichen: Stifter-Lektüren.* Stuttgart and Weimar: Metzler, 1995.

——. "'Realismus' oder 'Idealismus?' Über einige Schwierigkeiten bei der Rekonstruktion von Stifters Kunstbegriff." In *Adalbert Stifter: Dichter und Maler, Denkmalpfleger und Schulmann. Neue Zugänge zu seinem Werk.* Ed. Hartmut Laufhütte and Karl Möseneder. Tübingen: Niemeyer, 1996: 3–17.

Belgum, Kirsten L. "High Historicism and Narrative Restoration: The Seamless Interior of Adalbert Stifter's *Nachsommer.*" *Germanic Review* 67 (1992): 15–25.

Bertram, Ernst. *Studien zu Adalbert Stifters Novellentechnik.* Dortmund: Ruhfus, 1907.

——. "Nietzsche die Briefe Adalbert Stifters lesend." *Ariadne: Jahrbuch der Nietzsche-Gesellschaft* (1925): 7–26.

——. *Nietzsche: Versuch einer Mythologie.* Bonn: Bouvier, 1965, 247–58.

Blackall, Eric A. *Adalbert Stifter: A Critical Study.* Cambridge: Cambridge UP, 1948.

Bloch, Peter André. "Perspektive und Dimension: Die Textstruktur eines Wortgemäldes in Stifters *Nachsommer.*" *Études germaniques* 40 (1985): 281–96.

Böckmann, Paul. "Die epische Objektivität in Stifters Erzählung *Die Mappe meines Urgroßvaters*." In *Stoffe Formen Strukturen: Studien zur deutschen Literatur. Hans Heinrich Borcherdt zum 75. Geburtstag*. Ed. Albert Fuchs and Helmut Motekat. Munich: M. Hueber, 1962, 398–423.

Böhler, Michael. "Die Individualität in Stifters Spätwerk: Ein ästhetisches Problem." *Deutsche Vierteljahresschrift für Literaturwissenschaft und Geistesgeschichte* 43 (1969): 652–84.

Borchmeyer, Dieter. "Ideologie der Familie und ästhetische Gesellschaftskritik in Stifters *Nachsommer*." *Zeitschrift für deutsche Philologie* 99 (1980): 226–54.

Branscombe, Peter. "Some Reflections on the Use of Dialogue in Stifter's Stories." In *Adalbert Stifter heute: Londoner Symposium 1983*. Ed. Johann Lachinger, Alexander Stillmark, and Martin Swales. Linz: Adalbert-Stifter-Institut des Landes Oberösterreich, 1985, 12–23.

Brunner, Hans Ulrich. "Adalbert Stifter: Das Paradox des außerordentlich Ordentlichen." *VASILO* 37 (1988) 3/4: 11–38.

Büchner, Georg. *Sämtliche Werke und Briefe. Historisch-kritische Ausgabe*. Ed. Werner R. Lehmann. Munich: Hanser, 1974 (vol.1), 1972 (vol. 2).

Burger, Heinz Otto. "Der Stilwille der Unzeitgemäßen in Dichtung und Bildkunst des 19. Jahrhunderts." *Germanisch-Romanische Monatsschrift* 1 (1950–51): 289–96.

Campbell, Karen J. "Towards a Truer Mimesis: Stifter's *Turmalin*." *Germanic Quarterly* 57 (1984): 576–89.

Coleridge, Samuel Taylor. *Poems*. Ed. John Beer. London: Dent, 1986.

Dehn, Wilhelm. *Ding und Vernunft: Zur Interpretation von Stifters Dichtung*. Bonn: Bouvier, 1969.

Demetz, Peter. "Walter Benjamin als Leser Adalbert Stifters." In *Stifter Symposion: Vorträge und Lesungen*. Ed. Johann Lachinger. Linz: Linzer Veranstaltungsgesellschaft mbH and Adalbert-Stifter-Institut des Landes Oberösterreich, 1978, 38–43.

——. "On Stifter's and Fontane's Realism: *Turmalin* and *Mathilde Möhring*." In *Literary Criticism and Theory: "Festschrift" in Honor of René Wellek*. Ed. Joseph P. Strelka. Bern: Lang, 1984, 767–82.

Dettmering, Peter. "Eine Aura der Lautlosigkeit: Zum Bilde Adalbert Stifters." *Literatur und Kritik* 167/8 (1982): 68–72.

Domandl, Sepp. *Wiederholte Spiegelungen: Von Kant und Goethe bis Stifter*. Linz: Adalbert-Stifter-Institut des Landes Oberösterreich, 1982.

Doppler, Alfred. "Adalbert Stifters Verhältnis zur Geschichte." In *Stifter Symposion: Vorträge und Lesungen*. Ed. Johann Lachinger. Linz: Linzer Veranstaltungsgesellschaft mbH and Adalbert-Stifter-Institut des Landes Oberösterreich, 1978, 64–9.

——. "Formen und Möglichkeiten der wissenschaftlichen Stifter-Rezeption." In *Adalbert Stifter heute: Londoner Symposium 1983*. Ed. Johann Lachinger, Alexander Stillmark, and Martin Swales. Linz: Adalbert-Stifter-Institut des Landes Oberösterreich, 1985, 4–11.

——. "Hebbel und Stifter: Gegensätze und Gemeinsamkeiten." *VASILO* 34 (1985): 27–33.

——. "Schrecklich schöne Welt? Stifters fragwürdige Analogie von Natur- und Sittengesetz." In *Adalbert Stifters schrecklich schöne Welt: Beiträge des internationalen Kolloquiums zur A. Stifter-Ausstellung*. Ed. Roland Duhamel, Johann Lachinger, Clemens Ruthner, and Petra Göllner. Linz: Jahrbuch des Adalbert-Stifter-Institutes des Landes Oberösterreich, 1994, 9–15.

Duhamel, Roland. "Natur und Kunst: Zum didaktischen Konzept von Stifters *Nachsommer*." In *Adalbert Stifters schrecklich schöne Welt: Beiträge des internationalen Kolloquiums zur A. Stifter-Ausstellung*. Ed. Roland Duhamel, Johann Lachinger, Clemens Ruthner, and Petra Göllner. Linz: Jahrbuch des Adalbert-Stifter-Institutes des Landes Oberösterreich, 1994, 151–68.

Duhamel, Roland, Johann Lachinger, Clemens Ruthner, and Petra Göllner, eds. *Adalbert Stifters schrecklich schöne Welt: Beiträge des internationalen Kolloquiums zur A. Stifter-Ausstellung*. Linz: Jahrbuch des Adalbert-Stifter-Institutes des Landes Oberösterreich, 1994.

Ehlbeck, Birgit. "Zur poetologischen Funktionalisierung des Empirismus am Beispiel von Stifters *Kalkstein* und *Witiko*." In *Adalbert Stifter: Dichter und Maler, Denkmalpfleger und Schulmann. Neue Zugänge zu seinem Werk*. Ed. Hartmut Laufhütte and Karl Möseneder. Tübingen: Niemeyer, 1996: 455–75.

Eichinger, Ludwig M. "Beispiele einer Syntax der Langsamkeit: Aus Adalbert Stifters Erzählungen." In *Adalbert Stifter: Dichter und Maler, Denkmalpfleger und Schulmann. Neue Zugänge zu seinem Werk*. Ed. Hartmut Laufhütte and Karl Möseneder. Tübingen: Niemeyer, 1996, 246–60.

Eisenmeier, Eduard. "I. Nachtrag zu Stifters Werk in Amerika und England: Eine Bibliographie," *VASILO* 9 (1960): 129–32.

——. *Adalbert-Stifter-Bibliographie*. Linz: Oberösterreichischer Landesverlag and Adalbert-Stifter-Institut des Landes Oberösterreich, 1964.

——. *Adalbert-Stifter-Bibliographie: 1. Fortsetzung*. Linz: Oberösterreichischer Landesverlag and Adalbert-Stifter-Institut des Landes Oberösterreich, 1971.

——. *Adalbert-Stifter-Bibliographie: 2. Fortsetzung*. Linz: Oberösterreichischer Landesverlag and Adalbert-Stifter-Institut des Landes Oberösterreich, 1978.

——. *Adalbert-Stifter-Bibliographie: 3. Fortsetzung*. Linz. Oberösterreichischer Landesverlag and Adalbert-Stifter-Institut des Landes Oberösterreich, 1983.

Emrich, Wilhelm. *Franz Kafka*. Bonn: Athenäum, 1958.

Enzinger, Moriz. *Adalbert Stifters Studienjahre*. Innsbruck: Österreichische Verlagsanstalt, 1950.

——. *Gesammelte Aufsätze zu Adalbert Stifter*. Vienna: Österreichische Verlagsanstalt, 1967.

——. "Adalbert Stifters Erzählung *Zuversicht*." *VASILO* 17 (1968): 21–32.

——. *Adalbert Stifter im Urteil seiner Zeit: Festgabe zum 28. Jänner 1968*. Vienna: Böhlau, 1968.

——. "Verzeichnis der Literatur über A. Stifter 1840–1880." In Moriz Enzinger. *Adalbert Stifter im Urteil seiner Zeit*. Vienna: Böhlau (1968), 407–24.

Fischer, Kurt Gerhard. "Stifter und das Stifter-Bild." *VASILO* 9 (1960): 45–9.

——. "Versuch der Verständigung: Gedanken und Deutungen im Anschluß an Adalbert Stifters *Zuversicht*." *VASILO* 9 (1960): 94–105.

——. "Adalbert Stifter: Psychologische Beiträge zur Biographie." *VASILO* 10 (1961): 5–110.

——. *Adalbert Stifters Leben und Werk in Briefen und Dokumenten*. Frankfurt am Main: Fischer, 1962.

——. "Entwicklung und Bildung in Adalbert Stifters Dichten und Denken." *VASILO* 33 (1984): 53–60.

Freud, Sigmund. *Studienausgabe*. Ed. Alexander Mitscherlich, Angela Richards, and James Strachey. Frankfurt am Main: Fischer, 1982.

Frey, Bettina. "Die Änderungen Stifters im Manuskript B der Erzählung *Der fromme Spruch*." *VASILO* 19 (1970): 23–86.

Friedl, Hermann. "Maß und Ordnung." *VASILO* 11 (1962): 21–8.

Frischenschlager, Ruthilde. "Über Editionsschwierigkeiten des *Frommen Spruches*." *VASILO* 19 (1970): 11–22.

Fussenegger, Gertrud. "Utopie und Eros am Beispiel *Der Nachsommer*." In *Stifter Symposion: Vorträge und Lesungen*. Ed. Johann Lachinger. Linz: Linzer Veranstaltungsgesellschaft mbH and Adalbert Stifter Institut des Landes Oberösterreich, 1978, 87–90.

Gillespie, Gerald. "Ritualism and Motivic Development in Adalbert Stifter's *Der Nachsommer*." *Neophilologus* 48 (1964): 312–22.

——. "Space and Time Seen Through Stifter's Telescope." *Germanic Quarterly* 37 (1964): 120–30.

Glaser, Horst Albert. *Die Restauration des Schönen: Stifters "Nachsommer."* Stuttgart: Metzler, 1965.

——. "Auf Witikos Spuren: Stifters Schlachtenschilderungen." In *Adalbert Stifters schrecklich schöne Welt: Beiträge des internationalen Kolloquiums zur A. Stifter-Ausstellung.* Ed. Roland Duhamel, Johann Lachinger, Clemens Ruthner, and Petra Göllner. Linz: Jahrbuch des Adalbert-Stifter-Institutes des Landes Oberösterreich, 1994, 179–88.

Goodden, Christian. "Two Quests for Surety: A Comparative Interpretation of Stifter's *Abdias* and Kafka's *Der Bau.*" *Journal of European Studies* 5 (1975): 341–61.

Grasberger, Franz. "Adalbert Stifter und Anton Bruckner." In *Stifter Symposion: Vorträge und Lesungen.* Ed. Johann Lachinger. Linz: Linzer Veranstaltungsgesellschaft mbH and Adalbert Stifter Institut des Landes Oberösterreich, 1978, 48–55.

Grimm, Erk. "Vorspiel zum Glück: Heinrich Drendorfs *Nachsommer.*" *VASILO* 39 (1990) 3/4: 25–39.

Grimm, Jacob and Wilhelm. *Kinder- und Hausmärchen gesammelt durch die Brüder Grimm.* Munich: Winkler, 1990.

Grossmann Stone, Barbara S. *Adalbert Stifter and the Idyll: A Study of "Witiko."* New York, Bern, Frankfurt am Main, and Paris: Lang, 1990.

Gump, Margaret. *Adalbert Stifter.* New York: Twayne, 1974.

——. "Hesse über Stifter." *VASILO* 26 (1977): 13–16.

Haines, Brigid. *Dialogue and Narrative Design in the Works of Adalbert Stifter.* London: Modern Humanities Research Association, 1991.

——. "Dialog und Erzählstruktur in Stifters *Der Nachsommer.*" In *Adalbert Stifters schrecklich schöne Welt: Beiträge des internationalen Kolloquiums zur A. Stifter-Ausstellung.* Ed. Roland Duhamel, Johann Lachinger, Clemens Ruthner, and Petra Göllner. Linz: Jahrbuch des Adalbert-Stifter-Institutes des Landes Oberösterreich, 1994, 169–77.

Hebbel, Friedrich. *Werke.* Ed. Gerhard Fricke, Werner Keller, and Karl Pörnbacher. Munich: Hanser, 1965.

Hein, Alois Raimund. *Adalbert Stifter: Sein Leben und seine Werke.* Vienna: Walter Krieg, 1952.

Hein, Jürgen. "Bücher zum Stifter-Gedenkjahr 1968." *VASILO* 18 (1969): 47–70.

Hempel, Rainer L. "*Witiko* und die Kongruenz von Adalbert Stifters Gesamtwerk." *VASILO* 37 (1988) 1/2: 45–57.

Hesse, Hermann. *Gesammelte Werke.* Frankfurt am Main: Suhrkamp, 1976.

Hettche, Walter. "'. . . Die letzte Ausfeile ist das Feinste, und bedingt die Schönheit allein:' Stifters Arbeit an den *Bunten Steinen* und ihre Dokumentation in der *Historisch-Kritischen Gesamtausgabe*." In *Adalbert Stifters schrecklich schöne Welt: Beiträge des internationalen Kolloquiums zur A. Stifter-Ausstellung*. Ed. Roland Duhamel, Johann Lachinger, Clemens Ruthner, and Petra Göllner. Linz: Jahrbuch des Adalbert-Stifter-Institutes des Landes Oberösterreich, 1994, 77–85.

Hillebrand, Bruno. *Mensch und Raum im Roman: Studien zu Keller, Stifter, Fontane*. Munich: Winkler, 1971.

Hohoff, Curt. *Adalbert Stifter: Seine dichterischen Mittel und die Prosa des neunzehnten Jahrhunderts*. Düsseldorf: Schwann, 1949.

Höllerer, Walter. "Stifter." In Walter Höllerer. *Zwischen Klassik und Moderne: Lachen und Weinen in der Dichtung einer Übergangszeit*. Stuttgart: Klett, 1958, 357–77.

Hüller, Franz. *Adalbert Stifters "Witiko."* Nuremberg: Hans Carl, 1954.

Ingen, Ferdinand van. "Band und Kette: Zu einer Denkfigur bei Stifter." In *Adalbert Stifter: Dichter und Maler, Denkmalpfleger und Schulmann. Neue Zugänge zu seinem Werk*. Ed. Hartmut Laufhütte and Karl Möseneder. Tübingen: Niemeyer, 1996, 58–74.

Irmscher, Hans Dietrich. *Adalbert Stifter: Wirklichkeitserfahrung und gegenständliche Darstellung*. Munich: Fink, 1971.

——. "Phänomen und Begriff des Erhabenen im Werk Adalbert Stifters." *VASILO* 40 (1991) 3/4: 30–58.

Kafka, Franz. *Hochzeitsvorbereitungen auf dem Lande*. In Franz Kafka. *Gesammelte Werke*. Ed. Max Brod [Frankfurt am Main]: Fischer, 1953.

——. *Die Erzählungen*. [Frankfurt am Main]: Fischer, 1961.

——. *Das Schloß*. In Franz Kafka. *Gesammelte Werke*. Ed. Max Brod [Frankfurt am Main]: Fischer, 1964.

——. *Der Prozeß*. In Franz Kafka. *Gesammelte Werke*. Ed. Max Brod [Frankfurt am Main]: Fischer, 1965.

——. *Erzählungen*. In Franz Kafka. *Gesammelte Werke*. Ed. Max Brod [Frankfurt am Main]: Fischer, 1965.

——. *Tagebücher*. In Franz Kafka. *Schriften. Tagebücher. Briefe: Kritische Ausgabe*. Ed. Jürgen Born, Gerhard Neumann, Malcolm Pasley, and Jost Schillemeit [Frankfurt am Main]: Fischer, 1990.

Kaiser, Michael. "Stifters Dichtung als Quelle für die Erforschung seiner Kindheit und Jugend." In *Zur Literatur der Restaurationsepoche 1815–48: Friedrich Sengle zum 60. Geburtstag*. Ed. Jost Hermand and Manfred Windfuhr. Stuttgart: Metzler, 1970, 561–80.

——. *Adalbert Stifter: Eine literaturpsychologische Untersuchung seiner Erzählungen.* Bonn: Bouvier, 1971.

Kastner, Jörg. "Die Liebe im Werk Adalbert Stifters." In *Adalbert Stifter: Dichter und Maler, Denkmalpfleger und Schulmann. Neue Zugänge zu seinem Werk.* Ed. Hartmut Laufhütte and Karl Möseneder. Tübingen: Niemeyer, 1996, 119–34.

Keller, Gottfried. *Werke.* Zurich: Hanser, 1965.

Klatt, Fritz. "Stifter und das Dämonische." *Dichtung und Volkstum* 40 (1939): 276–95.

Knapp, Fritz Peter. "Mittelalterliche Herrschaftsideale und Stifters *Witiko.*" *VASILO* 40 (1991) 1/2: 63–73.

Koch, Franz. "Dichtung des Plunders." *Archiv für das Studium der neueren Sprachen* 186 (1949): 1–27.

——. "Stifter: existentiell." *VASILO* 2 (1953): 37–45.

Kosch, Wilhelm. *Adalbert Stifter und die Romantik.* Prague: Carl Bellmann, 1905.

Koschorke, Albrecht. "Das buchstabierte Panorama: Zu einer Passage in Stifters Erzählung *Granit.*" *VASILO* 38 (1989) 1/2: 3–13.

Koschorke, Albrecht, and Andreas Ammer. "Der Text ohne Bedeutung oder die Erstarrung der Angst: Zu Stifters letzter Erzählung *Der fromme Spruch.*" *Deutsche Vierteljahresschrift für Literaturwissenschaft und Geistesgeschichte* 61 (1987), 676–719.

Krökel, Fritz. "Nietzsches Verhältnis zu Stifter." *VASILO* 9 (1960): 106–20.

Kunisch, Hermann. *Adalbert Stifter: Mensch und Wirklichkeit. Studien zu seinem klassischen Stil.* Berlin: Duncker und Humblot, 1950.

——. "Die Ordnung des Seins bei Adalbert Stifter." In Hermann Kunisch. *Kleine Schriften.* Berlin and Munich: Duncker und Humblot, 1968, 357–71.

——. "*Witiko.*" In *Adalbert Stifter.* Ed. Lothar Stiehm. Heidelberg: Lothar Stiehm, 1968, 227–44.

Küpper, Peter. "Literatur und Langeweile: Zur Lektüre Stifters." In *Adalbert Stifter.* Ed. Lothar Stiehm. Heidelberg: Lothar Stiehm, 1968, 171–88.

Lachinger, Johann. "Mesmerismus und Magnetismus in Stifters Werk." In *Stifter Symposion: Vorträge und Lesungen.* Ed. Johann Lachinger. Linz: Linzer Veranstaltungsgesellschaft mbH and Adalbert Stifter Institut des Landes Oberösterreich, 1978, 16–23.

——, ed. *Stifter Symposion: Vorträge und Lesungen.* Linz: Linzer Veranstaltungsgesellschaft mbH and Adalbert Stifter Institut des Landes Oberösterreich, 1978. (= Proceedings of symposium held in conjunction with the International Bruckner Festival, Linz, 1978.)

Lachinger, Johann, and Martin Sturm, eds. *Adalbert Stifter: Schrecklich schöne Welt, VASILO* 39 (1990) 1/2 (= special publication on the occasion of the exhibition *Adalbert Stifter: Schrecklich schöne Welt* held in Krumau and Linz in 1990).

Lachinger, Johann, Alexander Stillmark, and Martin Swales, eds. *Adalbert Stifter heute: Londoner Symposium 1983*. Linz: Adalbert-Stifter-Institut des Landes Oberösterreich, 1985.

Laufhütte, Hartmut. "Zur Modernität eines Unmodernen: Anläßlich der Erzählung *Abdias* von Adalbert Stifter." In *Adalbert Stifters schrecklich schöne Welt: Beiträge des internationalen Kolloquiums zur A. Stifter-Ausstellung*. Ed. Roland Duhamel, Johann Lachinger, Clemens Ruthner, and Petra Göllner. Linz: Jahrbuch des Adalbert-Stifter-Institutes des Landes Oberösterreich, 1994, 65–75.

———. "Der *Nachsommer* als Vorklang der literarischen Moderne." In *Adalbert Stifter: Dichter und Maler, Denkmalpfleger und Schulmann. Neue Zugänge zu seinem Werk*. Ed. Hartmut Laufhütte and Karl Möseneder. Tübingen: Niemeyer, 1996, 486–507.

Laufhütte, Hartmut, and Karl Möseneder, eds. *Adalbert Stifter: Dichter und Maler, Denkmalpfleger und Schulmann. Neue Zugänge zu seinem Werk*. Tübingen: Niemeyer, 1996.

Lengauer, Hubert. "Konstitution und Selbstbeherrschung: Zum Verhältnis von Lebensgeschichte und Zeitgeschichte in Stifters *Mappe*." In *Adalbert Stifter heute: Londoner Symposium 1983*. Ed. Johann Lachinger, Alexander Stillmark, and Martin Swales. Linz: Adalbert-Stifter-Institut des Landes Oberösterreich, 1985, 135–49.

Lunding, Erik. *Adalbert Stifter: Mit einem Anhang über Kierkegaard und die existentielle Wissenschaft*. Copenhagen: Nyt Nordisk Forlag Arnold Busck, 1946.

———. "Forschungsbericht: Probleme und Ergebnisse der Stifterforschung 1945–1954." *Euphorion* 49 (1955): 203–44.

Mann, Thomas. *Briefe 1937–47*. Ed. Erika Mann. Frankfurt am Main: Fischer, 1963.

———. *Die Erzählungen*. In Thomas Mann. *Werke*. Frankfurt am Main and Hamburg: Fischer, 1967.

———. *Miszellen*. In Thomas Mann. *Werke*. Frankfurt am Main and Hamburg: Fischer, 1968.

———. *Schriften und Reden zur Literatur, Kunst und Philosophie*. In Thomas Mann. *Werke*. Frankfurt am Main and Hamburg: Fischer, 1968.

Markus, Andreas. *Der Tod Adalbert Stifters*. Neudeln: Ebering, 1967.

Mason, Eve. "Stifter's *Turmalin*: A Reconsideration." *Modern Language Review* 72 (1977): 348–58.

——. "Stifter's *Katzensilber* and the Fairy-tale Mode." *Modern Language Review* 77 (1982): 114–29.

——. "Stifters *Bunte Steine*: Versuch einer Bestandsaufnahme." In *Adalbert Stifter heute: Londoner Symposium 1983*. Ed. Johann Lachinger, Alexander Stillmark, and Martin Swales. Linz: Adalbert-Stifter-Institut des Landes Oberösterreich, 1985, 75–84.

——. *Stifter: "Bunte Steine."* London: Grant and Cutler, 1986.

Matz, Wolfgang. "Gewalt des Gewordenen: Adalbert Stifters Werk zwischen Idylle und Angst." *Deutsche Vierteljahresschrift für Literaturwissenschaft und Geistesgeschichte* 63 (1989): 715–50.

——. *Adalbert Stifter oder "Diese fürchterliche Wendung der Dinge."* Munich and Vienna: Hanser, 1995.

Meyer, Herman. *Der Sonderling in der deutschen Dichtung*. Munich: Hanser, 1963.

Müller, Heidy M. "'Ein Sturmwind über den Alpen Gottes:' Die Musik als apokalyptisches Medium des Unsagbaren in A. Stifters Erzählungen." In *Adalbert Stifters schrecklich schöne Welt: Beiträge des internationalen Kolloquiums zur A. Stifter-Ausstellung*. Ed. Roland Duhamel, Johann Lachinger, Clemens Ruthner, and Petra Göllner. Linz: Jahrbuch des Adalbert-Stifter-Institutes des Landes Oberösterreich, 1994, 105–17.

Müller, Joachim. "Wesenheit der Dinge." *VASILO* 3 (1954): 102–9.

——. "Einige Gestaltzüge in Stifters *Letzter Mappe*." In *Adalbert Stifter*. Ed. Lothar Stiehm. Heidelberg: Lothar Stiehm, 1968, 245–70.

——. "Stifters spätere Erzählungen." *VASILO* 9 (1979): 79–93.

——. "Das Furchtbare und großartig Erhabene: Adalbert Stifters Prosawerk *Aus dem Bairischen Walde*." *VASILO* 29 (1980): 122–38.

Muschg, Walter. *Tragische Literaturgeschichte*. Bern: Francke, 1948.

——. "Das Farbenspiel von Stifters Melancholie." In Walter Muschg. *Studien zur tragischen Literaturgeschichte*. Bern: Francke, 1965, 180–204.

Nemoianu, Virgil. "The Biedermeier Historical Novel." In Virgil Nemoianu. *European Literature and the Age of the Biedermeier*. Cambridge, Massachusetts, and London, 1984: Harvard UP, 214–32.

Nietzsche, Friedrich. *Menschliches, Allzumenschliches*. In Friedrich Nietzsche. *Werke*. Ed. Giorgio Colli and Mazzino Montinari. Berlin: de Gruyter, 1967, vol. 2.

Novotny, Fritz. *Adalbert Stifter als Maler*. Vienna: Schroll, 1941.

——. "Adalbert Stifters Zeichnungen aus den Lackenhäusern." In *Stifter Symposion: Vorträge und Lesungen*. Ed. Johann Lachinger. Linz: Linzer Veranstaltungsgesellschaft mbH and Adalbert Stifter Institut des Landes Oberösterreich, 1978, 13–15.

Oertel, Christine. "Stifters Erzählung *Der fromme Spruch*." *Monatshefte* 42 (1950): 231–6 (see also Sjögren, Christine Oertel).

Pascal, Roy. *The German Novel*. Manchester: Manchester UP, 1956.

Pawel, Ernst. *The Nightmare of Reason: A Life of Franz Kafka*. London, Glasgow, Sydney, Auckland, Toronto, and Johannesburg: Collins Harvil, 1988.

Pettersson, Torsten. "'Eine Welt aus Sehen und Blindheit:' Consciousness and World in Stifter's *Abdias*." *Germanisch-Romanische Monatsschrift* 40 (1990): 41–53.

Piechotta, Hans Joachim. *Aleatorische Ordnung*. Giessen: W. Schmitz, 1981.

Preisendanz, Wolfgang. "Die Erzählfunktion der Naturdarstellung bei Stifter." *Wirkendes Wort* 16 (1966): 407–18.

Ragg-Kirkby, Helena. "'Äußeres, Inneres, das ist alles eins:' Stifter's *Der Nachsommer* and the Problem of Perspectives." *German Life and Letters* 50 (1997): 323–38.

——. "'So ward die Wüste immer größer:' Zones of Otherness in the Stories of Adalbert Stifter." *Forum for Modern Language Studies* 35 (1999): 207–22.

——. "*Witiko* and the Absurd." In *The Biedermeier and Beyond. Selected Papers from the Symposium held at St. Peter's College, Oxford from 19–21 September 1997*. Ed. Ian F. Roe and John Warren. Bern, Berlin, Frankfurt am Main, New York, Paris, and Vienna: Lang, 1999, 169–81.

Reddick, John. "Tiger und Tugend in Stifters *Kalkstein*: Eine Polemik." *Zeitschrift für deutsche Philologie* 95 (1976): 235–55.

——. "Mystification, Perspectivism and Symbolism in *Der Hochwald*." In *Adalbert Stifter heute: Londoner Symposium 1983*. Ed. Johann Lachinger, Alexander Stillmark, and Martin Swales. Linz: Adalbert-Stifter-Institut des Landes Oberösterreich, 1985, 44–73.

——. "The Wild Beyond: Symbolic Journeyings in the Stories of Adalbert Stifter." *Oxford German Studies* 20/21 (1991–92): 104–24.

——. *Georg Büchner: The Shattered Whole*. Oxford: Oxford UP, 1994.

Reed, T. J. "The *Goethezeit* and its Aftermath." In *Germany: A Companion to German Studies*. Ed. Malcolm Pasley. London: Methuen, 1972, 493–553.

Reichart, Walter, and Werner H. Grilk, "Stifters Werk in Amerika und England: Eine Bibliographie." *VASILO* 9 (1960): 39–42.

Rey, W. H. "Das kosmische Erschrecken in Stifters Frühwerk." *Die Sammlung* 8 (1953): 6–13.

Ritchie, James Macpherson. *Periods in German Literature*. London: Wolff, 1968.

Ritter, Naomi. "Stifter und Kafka: Berührungspunkte." *VASILO* 27 (1978): 129–36.

Robertson, Ritchie. *Kafka: Judaism, Politics, and Literature.* Oxford: Oxford UP, 1987.

Roedl, Urban. *Adalbert Stifter: Geschichte seines Lebens.* Bern: Francke, 1958.

——. *Adalbert Stifter in Selbstzeugnissen und Bilddokumenten.* Reinbek bei Hamburg: Rowohlt, 1965.

Roget, Peter Mark. *Roget's Thesaurus of English Words and Phrases: New Edition Completely Revised and Modernised.* Ed. Robert A. Dutch. Longman: Harlow, 1962. (First published 1852).

Rosei, Peter. "Versuch über Stifter und einige Schriftsteller der Gegenwart." *Literatur und Kritik* 103 (1976): 161–7.

Rossbacher, Karlheinz. "Erzählstandpunkt und Personendarstellung bei Adalbert Stifter: Die Sicht von außen als Gestaltungsperspektive." *VASILO* 17 (1968): 47–58.

Rupp, Hans-Ulrich. *Stifters Sprache.* Zurich: Juris, 1969.

Sagarra, Eda. *Tradition and Revolution: German Literature and Society 1830–1890.* London: Weidenfeld and Nicolson, 1971.

Schäublin, Peter. "Familiales in Stifters *Nachsommer.*" In *Adalbert Stifter heute: Londoner Symposium 1983.* Ed. Johann Lachinger, Alexander Stillmark, and Martin Swales. Linz: Adalbert-Stifter-Institut des Landes Oberösterreich, 1985, 86–99.

Schorske, Carl Emil. *Fin-de-Siècle Vienna: Politics and Culture.* New York: Knopf, 1981.

Seidler, Herbert. "Die Natur in der Dichtung Stifters." *VASILO* 17 (1968): 223–39.

——. "Gestaltung und Sinn des Raumes in Stifters *Nachsommer.*" In *Adalbert Stifter.* Ed. Lothar Stiehm. Heidelberg: Lothar Stiehm, 1968, 203–26.

——. *Studien zu Grillparzer und Stifter.* Vienna, Cologne, and Graz: Böhlau, 1970.

——. "Zur Textfrage des *Frommen Spruches.*" *VASILO* 19 (1970): 10.

——. "Adalbert-Stifter-Forschung 1945–1970: Erster Teil." *Zeitschrift für deutsche Philologie,* 91 (1972): 113–57.

——. "Adalbert-Stifter-Forschung: Zweiter Teil." *Zeitschrift für deutsche Philologie* 91 (1972): 252–85.

——. "Adalbert Stifters späte Erzählkunst im Rahmen des bürgerlichen Realismus." In *Stifter Symposion: Vorträge und Lesungen.* Ed. Johann Lachinger. Linz: Linzer Veranstaltungsgesellschaft mbH and Adalbert Stifter Institut des Landes Oberösterreich, 1978, 44–7.

——. "Die Adalbert-Stifter-Forschung der siebziger Jahre." *VASILO* 30 (1981): 89–134.

Selge, Martin. *Adalbert Stifter: Poesie aus dem Geist der Naturwissenschaft.* Stuttgart: Kohlhammer, 1976.

——. "Stifters Kaktus: Zur naturwissenschaftlichen, (sexual-) symbolischen und ästhetischen Dimension des *Cereus Peruvianus* im *Nachsommer.*" In *Stifter Symposion: Vorträge und Lesungen.* Ed. Johann Lachinger. Linz: Linzer Veranstaltungsgesellschaft mbH and Adalbert Stifter Institut des Landes Oberösterreich, 1978, 28–37.

Sjögren, Christine Oertel. *The Marble Statue as Idea: Collected Essays on Adalbert Stifter's "Der Nachsommer."* Chapel Hill: North Carolina UP, 1972 (see also Oertel, Christine).

——. "Klotildes Reise in die Tiefe: Psychoanalytische Betrachtung zu einer Episode in Stifters *Nachsommer.*" *VASILO* 24 (1975): 107–11.

——. "Die 'gekränkte' Klotilde." *VASILO* 26 (1977): 39.

——. "Ein Musterbeispiel der Liebestheorie in Stifters *Nachsommer.*" *VASILO* 26 (1977): 111–15.

Small, Lauren. "White Frost Configurations on the Window Pane: Adalbert Stifter's *Der Nachsommer.*" *Colloquia Germanica* 18 (1985): 1–17.

Stahl, August. "Die ängstliche Idylle: Zum Gebrauch der Negationen in Stifters *Nachsommer.*" *Literatur und Kritik* 167/8 (1982): 19–28.

Staiger, Emil. *Adalbert Stifter als Dichter der Ehrfurcht.* Heidelberg: Lothar Stiehm, 1967.

——. "Reiz und Maß: Das Beispiel Stifters." In *Adalbert Stifter.* Ed. Lothar Stiehm. Heidelberg: Lothar Stiehm, 1968, 7–22.

Stern, J. P. *Reinterpretations: Seven Studies in Nineteenth Century German Literature.* London: Thames and Hudson, 1964.

——. "Adalbert Stifters ontologischer Stil." In *Adalbert Stifter.* Ed. Lothar Stiehm. Heidelberg: Lothar Stiehm, 1968, 103–20.

——. *Idylls and Realities: Studies in Nineteenth Century German Literature.* London: Methuen, 1971.

——. "*Der Nachsommer* und *Das Glasperlenspiel*: Probleme der ästhetischen Provinz." In *Stifter Symposion: Vorträge und Lesungen.* Ed. Johann Lachinger. Linz: Linzer Veranstaltungsgesellschaft mbH and Adalbert Stifter Institut des Landes Oberösterreich, 1978, 80–6.

Stiehm, Lothar, ed. *Adalbert Stifter: Studien und Interpretationen.* Heidelberg: Lothar Stiehm, 1968.

Stillmark, Alexander. "Stifter's Symbolism of Beauty: The Significance of the Flower in his Works." *Oxford German Studies* 6 (1972): 74–92.

——. "Stifter's *Letzte Mappe* and the Idea of Wholeness." In *Tradition and Creation: Essays in Honour of E. M. Wilkinson.* Ed. C. P. Magill, B. A. Rowley, and C. J. Smith. Leeds: Maney, 1978, 162–76.

——. "Stifter and Wordsworth: Observations on some Affinities in Creative Imagination." In *Adalbert Stifter heute: Londoner Symposium 1983.* Ed. Johann Lachinger, Alexander Stillmark, and Martin Swales. Linz: Adalbert-Stifter-Institut des Landes Oberösterreich, 1985, 25–35.

——. "Per aspera ad astra: The Secret Insignia of Stifter's *Nachsommer.*" *Publications of the English Goethe Society* 59 (1988–89): 79–98.

Stockum, Th. C. van. "*Die Mappe meines Urgroßvaters* und ihre Bedeutung im Zusammenhang von Stifters Werk und Weltanschauung." *Neophilologus* 30 (1946): 172–84.

Stopp, Frederick. "Die Symbolik in Stifters *Bunten Steinen.*" *Deutsche Vierteljahresschrift für Literaturwissenschaft und Geistesgeschichte* 28 (1954), 165–73.

Storck, Joachim W. "Stifter und Rilke." In *Adalbert Stifter.* Ed. Lothar Stiehm. Heidelberg: Lothar Stiehm, 1968, 271–302.

——. "'Unter Witikos Banner?' Bemerkungen zu Adalbert Stifters böhmischem Geschichtsbild." In *Stifter Symposion: Vorträge und Lesungen.* Ed. Johann Lachinger. Linz: Linzer Veranstaltungsgesellschaft mbH and Adalbert Stifter Institut des Landes Oberösterreich, 1978, 70–9.

Swales, Erika. "The Doubly Woven Text: Reflections on Stifter's Narrative Mode." In *Adalbert Stifter heute: Londoner Symposium 1983.* Ed. Johann Lachinger, Alexander Stillmark, and Martin Swales. Linz: Adalbert-Stifter-Institut des Landes Oberösterreich, 1985, 37–43.

Swales, Martin. *The German "Novelle."* Princeton: Princeton UP, 1977.

——. *The German "Bildungsroman" from Wieland to Hesse.* Princeton: Princeton UP, 1978.

——. "Litanei und Leerstelle: Zur Modernität Adalbert Stifters." *VASILO* 36 (1987) 3/4: 71–82.

Swales, Martin, and Erika Swales. *Adalbert Stifter: A Critical Study.* Cambridge: Cambridge UP, 1984.

Vancsa, Kurt. "Neue Stifter-Literatur." *VASILO* 5 (1956): 27–31.

Walter-Schneider, M. "Das Unrecht des Wählens: Bemerkungen zu Stifters spätem Stil." *Wirkendes Wort* 32 (1982): 267–75.

——. "Der Erzähler auf dem Weg: Über ein Motivwandel im Werk Adalbert Stifters." *Zeitschrift für deutsche Philologie* 107 (1988): 212–33.

Ward, John Owen (ed.). *The Oxford Companion to Music.* Oxford: Oxford UP, 1992. (First published 1938).

Watanabe-O'Kelly, Helen. "Stifters *Waldsteig*: Sexuelle Erziehung eines Narren." In *Adalbert Stifter heute: Londoner Symposium 1983.* Ed. Johann Lachinger, Alexander Stillmark, and Martin Swales. Linz: Adalbert-Stifter-Institut des Landes Oberösterreich, 1985, 121–34.

——, trans. *Adalbert Stifter: "Brigitta" and Other Tales.* London: Penguin, 1994.

Weippert, Georg. *Stifters "Witiko": Vom Wesen des Politischen.* Munich: Verlag für Geschichte und Politik, 1967.

Whitinger, Raleigh. "Elements of Self-Consciousness in Adalbert Stifter's *Der Nachsommer.*" *Colloquia Germanica* 23 (1990): 241–52.

Wiesmüller, Wolfgang. "Schreiben zwischen Flucht und Widerstand: Adalbert Stifters Arbeit am *Witiko.*" *VASILO* 40 (1991) 1/2: 46–62.

——. "'Wann werden Völker Völker sein?' Zeitgemäße und unzeitgemäße Betrachtungen Adalbert Stifters zur Lage Europas." In *Adalbert Stifters schrecklich schöne Welt: Beiträge des internationalen Kolloquiums zur A. Stifter-Ausstellung.* Ed. Roland Duhamel, Johann Lachinger, Clemens Ruthner, and Petra Göllner. Linz: Jahrbuch des Adalbert-Stifter-Institutes des Landes Oberösterreich, 1994, 189–97.

Wildbolz, Rudolf. *Adalbert Stifter: Langeweile und Faszination.* Stuttgart: Kohlhammer, 1976.

Winkler, Christian. "Die Änderungen Stifters im Manuskript B der Erzählung *Der fromme Spruch.*" *VASILO* 19 (1970): 87–117.

Winterstein, Alfred. *Adalbert Stifter: Persönlichkeit und Werk. Eine tiefenpsychologische Studie.* Vienna: Phönix, 1946.

Wodtke, Friedrich Wilhelm. "Mensch und Schicksal in Stifters frühen *Studien.*" *Wirkendes Wort* 12 (1962): 12–28.

Wyder, Margrit. "Vorhof zum Tempel: Der Anfang von Stifters *Nachsommer.*" *Sprachkunst* 20 (1989): 149–75.

Index

D1599002